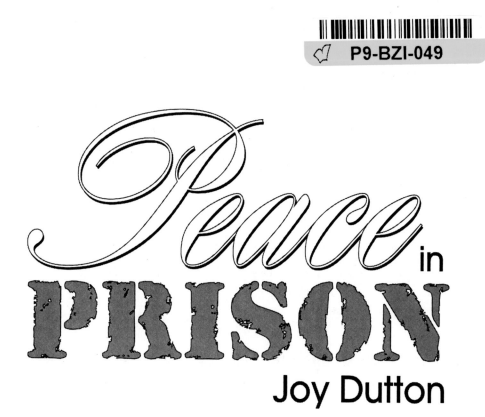

Peace in PRISON

Joy Dutton

*Pray,
Read &
Share

Joy Dutton*

TEACH Services, Inc.
P U B L I S H I N G
www.TEACHServices.com

Copyright © 2012 Joy Dutton & TEACH Services, Inc.
ISBN-13: 978-1-57258-817-2 (Paperback)
ISBN-13: 978-1-57258-818-9 (Hardback)
ISBN-13: 978-1-57258-819-6 (ePub)
ISBN-13: 978-1-57258-820-2 (Kindle/Mobi)
Library of Congress Control Number: 2012937801

Published by

TEACH Services, Inc.
P U B L I S H I N G
www.TEACHServices.com

Table of Contents

Prison and Prayer

In the *Wizard of Oz,* Dorothy was in her own black-and-white prison. As she sang "Somewhere Over the Rainbow," her imagination took her on a colorful and exciting adventure. When she arrived back in Kansas, with the people she knew and loved, to the farm that once was dull to her, she admitted, "There's no place like home."

A mother of three small children complained, "Will I never get enough sleep again?" She wanted her youngest to be able to walk, so she didn't have to carry the load. Her prison was in a land of children. She, like Dorothy, couldn't see the beauty of what she had—three normal, active, healthy, amusing, needy and, if she would notice, very loving children.

My friend Bob had a knee replaced. In the hospital two days after the surgery, he needed a visitor, so I went to see him. He was in miserable pain, and his groans were so constant that I realized his hospital bed was his prison. But nothing lasts forever. Bob finally recovered, and he lived to dance once again with his lovely wife, a joy he never expected to experience again.

The day after I visited Bob in the hospital, I visited another friend. Another Bob. Another place. I'll call him Bob #2, as he was wearing a number on his chest. His number was too long for me to remember, but I'll never forget Bob #2.

When the jailer threw Bob #2 into the cell, he fell to his knees and crumpled down as far as a human being can get, and he prayed—actually groaned—"God, oh God, what have I done?"

What is your prison? What is holding you there? What is the release that finally gives peace to the troubled and twisted heart? Or is there a way out? Is prison just a place or is it an attitude we all encase ourselves in? Can something or someone help you in your prison? Can you find your way out of your prison?

Talking with your Creator God seems to be the very first step out. If, like Dorothy, the mother, and the two Bobs, you are searching for release from your prison, lift your face to the heavens and ask God to take your hand in His hand. He will lead you out of your prison into a peace that you have never known. It's that simple. He will answer. Just do it.

Jesus in Jail

Prayer was all Bob #2 had going for him. His cellmates hated him and threatened to kill him first chance they could. Indeed, in a fight, he got his lip busted and two front teeth knocked out. He was a small man, defenseless, scared, and severely lonely.

Soon after his arrest, Bob's wife invited me visit him in jail. He was my neighbor. How could I refuse? During our first visit, he hung his head, covered his face with his hands, and mumbled, "I didn't do it." He never said another word, but the shame and guilt poured from his very being. Later he was found guilty of 20 counts, which he finally admitted to doing.

Counseling, visits, and nine years spent in prison did nothing to change Bob #2's life. He didn't really want God. He never got out of his own prison because he chose to ignore God. He stopped praying. What a tragedy. However, Bob #2 still has life. His original groan of a prayer—"God, oh God, what have I done?"—may someday have its effect on his life. I am praying it will. You see, he was my neighbor.

What does prayer do that nothing else will ever do? It connects you to your Creator. God made you, and Jesus Christ died for your life of sin—He redeemed you on a horrible cross one Friday many years ago. And He is coming back to take you out of this prison of sin called earth to a home in heaven where sin and crime will no longer exist.

Heaven is not "pie in the sky." Heaven is a real place. It is where God lives. He is inviting you to get ready. He's coming back soon to take you home with Him. The Holy Scriptures is God's letter of invitation to live with Him.

But do we have to wait till He comes to have that heaven? No, we can have God in our hearts this very moment if we want Him. Just ask Him into your heart. He will turn your life around. He has done this for millions before. His door is always open.

He calls Himself the Good Shepherd. He has looked after you all your life, whether you know it or not. Now He is inviting you to accept Him and to fill your heart with His peace. Tell Him your life's struggles. He may be invisible, but He is real, and He wants to give you peace. Ask Him. Receive His peace. Know you are free, no matter what "jail" you are in.

Home-Bound

I have another friend in jail. He was actually a student of mine. Teaching music has always been my passion, and students are my love. He was easy to love—funny, handsome, good voice. When he called from jail, my heart hurt deeply. So I traveled to jail and visited him. We had a good talk, but he was not willing to release his past, to reach out to his Creator for the peace he wants. He hangs on to a life of misery he doesn't need to live in.

When he was still a boy, he told me, "Joy, I'm heaven-bound." And I know he meant it then. Now, he's saying, "I don't want heaven; I've had it with God." Oh, if he would only let go of the past and reach out his hand to God, he would find peace—the very thing that eludes him.

Heaven-bound. Where is it? What is it? Can anyone go? Am I too far away from God? Will He have me after all I've done? Well, let's see.

God's Word tells us in 1 John 1:9 that "if we confess our sins,he is faithful and just and will forgive us our sins" (NIV). That's pretty plain. To confess our sins is simply telling God what He knows anyway. You can't fool God. He knows everything about you. He made you. He loves you. And oh how He longs to hear your voice telling Him what you have done.

Heaven used to be "my goal" in life. But one day I realized that heaven is God's home. Heaven is a place. It's really God that I want. And God wants me. Now my goal is God. You see, if God is my greatest desire, I have Him. He's always there beside me—He's always there beside you. He is not locked out by clanging doors, gates, or barbed wire. He's always with you.

King David tells us in Psalm 37:4, "Delight yourself in the Lord and he will give you the desires of your heart" (NIV).

Long ago I chose to desire Jesus Christ. And I have Him. No, I'm not a perfect human being, but I wish all people had the peace of the presence of God that I have.

No matter what is going on, good, bad, or worse still, God has given me His presence, and all things are OK when He is there. Each day I ask for His presence. He gives liberally. I've accepted. Friend, you, too, can have this peace.

Innocent

Joseph was framed. While sitting in prison, he must have asked God why he was accused when he was innocent.

Prior to becoming a slave he had lived in elegance. As his father's favorite son, he was pampered beyond reason. As his brothers tended the sheep, he lived a life of luxury.

One day his father said, "Go and see how your brothers and the flocks are doing" (Gen. 37:14, *The Message*; see Gen. 37-50 for the rest of the story). Joseph obeyed his father. But when his brothers saw him coming, they decided to kill him. But first they threw him in a pit. Then, as luck would have it, a camel train of Ishmaelites drew near. So they lifted him out of the pit and sold him to these strangers for 20 pieces of silver. And off he went into a strange land.

Potiphar, the king's officer, bought Joseph at the slave market. Working as a slave for Potiphar, Joseph did a good job. He was promoted until Joseph was in charge of everything Potiphar owned.

So far, so good. But Potiphar had a wife who wanted Joseph to be her lover. He resisted, saying, "How can I sin against God?" After several attempts to entice him, Potiphar's wife grabbed his coat. He wiggled himself out of it and ran from her presence.

Then she had the nerve to blame him for raping her. Potiphar ordered Joseph to be put in prison. There he was, in prison for a crime he did *not* do. I'm sure he had time to question God about his predicament.

I'm certain he had to deal with some feelings of resentment toward his hateful brothers. And I'm certain he wondered why, when he was a child of God, He hadn't protected him from such violent treatment.

In the Holy Scriptures where this story is told you can read about what God did for Joseph. God had a plan. This is one of the most beautiful stories of letting God lead. First, Joseph was placed in charge of the prisoners. Two years later after his release from prison he was made governor over all the land of Egypt. He saved Egypt from starvation through interpreting dreams God sent to Pharaoh.

Then Joseph had the opportunity to feed his brothers who had traveled from their home in Israel to Egypt in search of food. Joseph, who was next to the highest in the land, stood tall while his brothers bowed down to him in respect. What a twist of fate for a 17-year-old prisoner.

Escaped

Peter sat on the cold prison floor chained to two soldiers. King Herod had warned him not to speak in public about this "Messiah" he kept preaching about. They warned him that the next time he spoke about Jesus he would be locked up.

But Peter could not keep his mouth shut. After all, he had lived for three years with the Messiah, and he wanted everyone to know his Lord. How could he keep his mouth shut? And the other disciples were telling everyone they could about this Messiah the Jews had been looking for. So he spoke up.

The prophets all told of the future Messiah. They explained that He would be born in Bethlehem of a virgin mother who had conceived by the Holy Spirit. The time, place, and situation of His birth were well documented in the Old Testament by the prophets who wrote what God told them to write.

Peter, who was human and always getting into some trouble till he finally got it right, was now doing the very thing he *had to* do. And he found himself in prison for doing good.

As he sat there, his thoughts were on his Savior, the very Messiah he spent so many days and nights with. A quiet peace filled his heart. He finally went to sleep. Suddenly an angel of God shook him awake and said, "Shh, follow me." Peter thought it was only a dream, but he followed the angel anyway.

When he sat up, the chains fell from his arms. He was free to walk around. He followed the angel. They walked past the guards, and the outside gate swung open. Shortly after they exited the prison, the angel left. Then Peter realized he was free. So he walked to his friend's house. John Mark, another friend of the Messiah, had a lot of fellow believers over for a prayer session for Peter's safety.

Now, here's the funny part of the story. You can read about it in the Good Book. As he knocked, a young maid named Rhoda came to the door. When she heard Peter's voice, she ran inside telling the people Peter was there. So excited, she didn't open the door.

Peter was left standing alone while Rhoda told the others, "Peter is at the door." Finally, someone opened the door, and the rest is history (Acts 12:1-19).

In a Dungeon

God chose a special man to do a special work for Him. After Jesus died on the cross, the good news about His resurrection and ascension to heaven had to be told.

Although Jesus was a Jew, the rest of the world (known as the Gentiles) needed to hear this truth. And God handpicked Paul to do the telling. By and by it got him into trouble, and he ended up in prison in Rome, Italy. The remarkable thing was that being locked up gave Paul time to write to the new believers.

Here are some marvelous gems Paul sent to the converts in Philippi, which are recorded in the book of Philippians in the New Testament.

Being confident of this very thing, that He which hath begun a good work in you will perform it until the day of Jesus Christ (chapter 1, verse 6).

For to me to live is Christ, and to die is gain (chapter 1, verse 21).

For it is God which works in you both to will and to do of His good pleasure (chapter 2, verse 13).

Forgetting those things which are behind, and reaching forth unto those things which are before, I press toward the mark for the prize of the high calling of God in Christ Jesus (chapter 3, verses 13, 14).

Rejoice in the Lord always: and again I say, Rejoice (chapter 4, verse 4).

And the peace of God, which passes all understanding, shall keep your hearts and minds through Christ Jesus (chapter 4, verse 7).

For I have learned, in whatsoever state I am, therewith to be content (chapter 4, verse 11).

I can do all things through Christ which strengthens me (chapter 4, verse 13).

But my God shall supply all your needs according to His riches in glory by Christ Jesus (chapter 4, verse 19).

Imagine a man in a dungeon "rejoicing" in the Lord. Listen to what Paul writes in Philippians 1:13: "All the soldiers here, and everyone else, too, found out that I'm in jail because of this Messiah. That piqued their curiosity, and now they've learned all about him" (*The Message*).

True Independence

Independence Day is celebrated by all U.S. citizens in a big way. From tiny firecrackers to the bombs bursting in air, each town and community shares in the thrill of independence. Celebrating with flare and flame, we keep alive the excitement of that first Independence Day, July 4, 1777.

Most countries celebrate their independence from another country's control. Wars are fought with independence in mind. Victories yield joyous shouts for a land that's at last free. Yet, more war go on. Is there always a battle to fight before freedom rings? Apparently so. The Bible suggests that we must "fight the good fight" (1 Tim. 6:12). What is a spiritual fight, and how does it bring about independence?

Long ago, before the world was created, there was a battle in heaven. God, Jesus Christ, and the Holy Spirit created the angels as perfect beings. There was harmony in heaven, and as God continued creating planets, small and large, the angels watched and sang songs of rejoicing at each new and wonderful act of their Creator.

However, for some reason, the choir director became jealous of his own Creator, and Lucifer caused an uproar in heaven. At first, he did some undercover work. Finally, in a battle with God Himself, he was cast out of heaven.

The newest planet created was earth, and so Lucifer the angel became Satan the devil. It is a mystery how this could come about, but it did. And there had to be a way out of the mess Satan made of planet earth.

Indeed, the Lord promised Adam and Eve their independence through the Son of God who would one day die on the cross for their freedom from Satan. About two thousand years ago, Jesus died for our true independence, freedom from the clutches of the devil. We are free by accepting Jesus' gift of salvation.

"For God so loved the world, that he gave his only begotten Son, that whosoever believeth in him should not perish, but have everlasting life. For God sent not his Son into the world to condemn the world; but that the world through him might be saved" (John 3:16, 17).

Now, that's true *independence* from the devil, the worst enemy ever. Believe in the Son of God—that's *freedom*.

Before the King

Esther stood silently at the far side of the king's throne room. He had not summoned her. In the kingdom it was law to be summoned before entering the king's throne room. But there she stood, tall, beautiful, waiting.

The moment of truth for her life seemed like an eternity. She waited, and as the king finally focused on his lovely wife, he held out his scepter toward her. So far, so good.

Queen Esther was a Jewess. Her ancestry was from Israel, not from the country where her people were held captive. The circumstances under which she became a queen in this foreign country were unheard of before in all the history of the world.

The Babylonians had captured her people, the Jews, many years before. For the most part, the Jews lived peacefully in Babylonia. Yet they longed to return to their Promised Land, Israel. However, God knew an incident would arise, and he prepared a Jewish maid to deliver her people.

King Ahasuerus had been married to the beautiful Queen Vashti. But he had dethroned her and divorced her on the spot when she wouldn't come out and dance for the people at one of the king's banquets, even though he ordered her to do so.

Realizing he needed a wife now, he had all the beauties in the land brought to the palace for a sort of "Miss America Pageant." Esther was among the beautiful maidens. She kept quiet about being a Jewess.

Esther was chosen to be the king's new wife. All would have been well, but she had a cousin, Mordecai, who worked as a guard at the gate of the kingdom. And the bad guy in the story, Haman, expected Mordecai to bow to him, but being a Jew, Mordecai would only bow to God—the Creator of the universe. He considered Haman to be just an ordinary fellow, a created being. Only God should have his honor. This infuriated Haman. So Haman, knowing Mordecai was a Jew, took an idea to the king. The king then made a law and sealed it with his own ring.

He proposed that all the Jews in the land be eliminated. Mordecai sent a message to Esther. Her bravery by confronting both the king and Haman is on record in the book of Esther. A thrilling book to read of loyalty to God and bravery for her own people. Standing up to the king required her to be very brave indeed.

Running, Always Running

The king did not like David. In fact he raged with jealousy. God had chosen David to be King Saul's successor. Also, David slew ten thousands in battle, while King Saul only had victory over thousands.

Playing his harp for King Saul, David learned to dodge a javelin, as well as to pluck the strings to soothe the king's wild emotions. At last, David had to flee for his life.

Hiding in caves with his soldier companions, David knew his life was in jeopardy. Once while David and his men were deep in a cave, King Saul entered. David had the advantage. His men said, "Let's get him." But being true to his God, and honoring the king, he restrained his men from killing Saul. Instead, David cut off a corner of Saul's robe and, at a safe distance, called to Saul, holding up the cloth.

Another time when Saul was sleeping and David was hiding in another cave, David took Saul's spear and his water jug, walked across the valley, and then shouted, "King, O King, where is your spear?" The king had to admit that David was the better man.

Running, running, running, always running to escape for his life, David spent many years in terrible torment. Reading the psalms in the Holy Scriptures, you can feel his fear. Yet, through it all, he found time to communicate with his Maker. He wrote psalms about his confidence in the Lord—no matter what.

Psalm 18:29 describes how David felt as God guided him. "For by thee I have run through a troop; and by my God I have leaped over a wall." Can't you imagine David holding on to God's hand and running from Saul as hard and fast as feet could take him?

Early in David's life, he was a shepherd boy. His confidence in his God was well intact before his first encounter with King Saul; that's why he could say with assuredness, "Thou hast enlarged my steps under me; so that my feet did not slip" (2 Samuel 22:37).

Do you ever feel as if you've been running and running for a long time? Take courage from David. Say with him: "I count on God as my Rock, my Deliverer, my God, my Strength."

Someone once said, "God comes alongside us when we go through hard times, and before you know it, He brings us alongside someone else who is going through hard times so that we can be there for that person just as God was there for us." I have experienced this, and so can you.

Thrown in the Den

Daniel was a man of impeccable righteousness. Daniel was a Jew who was captured by the Babylonians around 606 BC, along with his friends, Shadrach, Meshach, and Abednego.

Once captured, Daniel decided in his heart to eat pure food. As soon as they entered the king's palace, they requested water and "pulse" (vegetables). Melzar, the servant in charge of the trainees, was horrified. He could not disobey the king. You see, the king had ordered rich food for all the potential wise men.

Daniel suggested a testing period of ten days. After eating the simple food for the allotted period of time, the servant found "their countenance ... fairer and fatter in flesh" (Dan. 1:15). Later, the king also found Daniel and his friends to be fairer than all the other captives.

Daniel fared well. In fact, he rose higher in the kingdom until he was chief over the officers of the land. Unfortunately, those under him grew jealous of him. They wanted his place in the kingdom, so they set traps for him. Day after day, Daniel showed his purity by his manners, his fairness in business, and his courtesy to others. There was not cause for his being punished.

But jealousy hung on tenaciously, and they finally found one thing they could "get him" for. Daniel opened his windows and prayed three times a day. Ah-ha! They had him cornered. So they presented a law against worshipping "other gods" than the king for thirty days.

How many of us would have simply closed the window to talk to God? But that's the coward's way out. Daniel did not do that. He kept his window open, and he prayed.

Once he was trapped, the jealous men presented this fact to the king. Now the king realized *he* was trapped. He had sealed a bad law with his own signet ring, and the law could not be reversed. He waited all day, hoping for a way out. He knew of Daniel's upright character, his honesty and integrity. Now he was trapped into killing a good man.

The den, deep in the earth, was full of lions. They threw Daniel in. Very early the next morning the king arrived at the den and asked Daniel, "Is thy God ... able to deliver thee from the lions?" Oh, yes. Daniel said, "My God ... hath shut the lions' mouths" (Dan. 6:20, 22).

We have a great God who can do anything. Few of us are pure as Daniel, but wherever we are, we can choose to serve Daniel's God. Who knows when we will need help from our God?

A Can of Beans

It was the day before Thanksgiving, and payday was five days away. I had recently gotten a divorce, and I was hurting. I suppose I was having a pity party all my own when the doorbell rang.

Opening the door just a crack, I gazed into my minister's wife's beaming face. *How nice to see a good friend*, I thought. So I invited her in, and we chatted for a while. Then, trying to be a good hostess, I asked if she wanted to look around my "home"—a very modest two-room home plus a bathroom.

She could see my main room, which consisted of a kitchen, dining room, living room. It was very small, but adequate for my few things. Next, showing her my tiny bedroom with a sewing machine, an exerciser, dresser, and a tight space for a bed, we laughed at how possible it really is for someone to manage in a small space.

Next I took her into the hallway leading to the bathroom. I opened up the closet doors and fairly gushed at all the space and the many cupboards that held everything I owned. We briefly checked out the bathroom before returning to the living room, dining room, kitchen, and pantry, which was all in one room. I pointed out my "music room." Yes, there was room for my piano and a set of drawers for my music. We continued as I reviewed a promise from God in Philippians 4:19: "My God shall supply all your need."

As I was showing her the kitchen, I opened up the pantry door. But it was too late; she saw inside—there was one can of beans sitting on one lone shelf. Our eyes met. "Oh, it's OK. I'm just about to get paid again, and my pantry will be filled to the brim," I said. I was trying so hard to be lighthearted. After she left I got my Bible out and re-read Romans 8:28, "And we know that all things work together for good to them that love God."

A little while later the doorbell rang again. There she was. This time she had a big box full of groceries.

I cannot fully explain my feelings at that moment. She said, "The church ladies made up a few boxes, and we thought you could use one of them."

"Oh, I'm so EMBARRASSED," I said.

"We knew you would be," she said. Then she left.

Looking through the box, I was delighted to discover that *all* the food was on my food plan—I wasn't allergic to anything in that box. Then the doorbell rang again. This time she held a second box. Glancing at the food, I said, "I'm so thankful!"

"We knew you would be," she said. God *does* supply our need.

A Jewish Journey

Two people and a donkey struck out on a 90-mile journey one day in Israel. They were not alone. The entire country traveled, also. The governor had declared a tax to be paid in the place of their birth, so these two traveled, along with the rest of the people of the land, were making their way to their hometown.

The only difference was that they traveled slower, more cautiously, than the rest. They had packed their very meager belongings carefully—food, some clothes, and cloth to wrap a baby in, for indeed they had a new baby with them. The unborn Child rode along in His mother's womb, for He was waiting for the right place to be born.

Many years before this journey prophets told of this very birth, the birth of the Savior of the world. Prophecy specifically mentioned Bethlehem. Well, the couple lived in Nazareth, 90 miles away from Bethlehem. And if the governor had not demanded tax in their original city of birth, they would not have taken such a perilous trip (Micah 5:2; Matt. 2:1; Luke 2:4).

Just imagine as they packed their meager baggage for the next part of the journey. How concerned the father, Joseph, must have been for his delicate wife. Just imagine how tentatively Mary, the mother, must have climbed on the donkey's back. Picture in your mind's eye the dusty trail, Joseph's sore feet, Mary's aching back. Feel the tiredness as each day blended in with the other days on the journey.

Group after group must have passed them wishing them Godspeed. But Joseph and Mary had to take their time while still moving forward. I wonder what loneliness and fear must have crept into their minds as they took one painful and fearful step after another. Did they wonder why God allowed this tax demand at such a time as this?

As they neared Jerusalem, probably traveling through it to get to Bethlehem, their desired destiny, what emotions must have welled up in their throats as they saw the glory of the temple and the other beautiful buildings. Yet, they plodded on.

Once they arrived in Bethlehem, they traveled from inn to inn. They kept hearing "no vacancy" from many places. Finally, after all the village inns were checked out, they came to an innkeeper who felt a generous tug on his heart. He offered his barn as a place for the night. Little did he know that the Savior of the world would be born that night. This was the end of their journey, and the beginning of our salvation.

The Longest Journey
Part 1

I want you to imagine Jesus hanging on the cross and thinking about His journey:

"Here I am hanging on a cross. My hands are nailed to a wooden beam. There is one nail thrust through both feet. Blood is dripping from My head. A thorny crown has been smashed into My head. Spit is dribbling from My face. My back is torn to shreds by an unmerciful beating. Mocking and jeering, the mob looks on. Why do I hang here? Because I love My people, all of them, including those who are crucifying Me.

"I am halfway into the longest journey. Let Me tell you the story. The beginning of My journey was in a perfect setting. My Father, His Spirit, and Myself held a conference about creating a new planet. This had to be a secret committee. We planned it alone. We didn't need help or suggestions.

"As We planned to create a new planet, We discussed the possibility of something going wrong. Up until now everything in Our home was perfect. Heaven was just that—*heaven*. With myriads of angels, each one had a position in the celestial home, each one was entirely satisfied with life as it was. My Father, Myself, and the Spirit of God were content. We are called the Trinity, the Godhead, three in one—one God. We longed to create a world and populate it. That was the theme of this private conference.

"Because the law of the universe was and is love, We created angels with the power of choice. Can you imagine the delight God had while creating? But the natural outcome of this perfect love is what caused a problem. However, creating automatons without freedom of choice would have been infinitely worse. Can you imagine the sorrow God had when something did go wrong.

"Once the meeting was over, and I stepped down from My Father's throne, I was met by the highest angel of all. He had a face of discontent. He was jealous of Me. You see, I had a conference with the Father without inviting him. That was strange because he was a mere created being. My Father, Myself, and the Spirit have always existed. We have *no* beginning. We created him, yet he was jealous of Me.

"This discontent of the highest angel spread to other angels like a virus of the worst kind. Lucifer was his name. He finally influenced one third of the angels to join him in rebellion against God, and they went to make war with the Most High God.

"However, in the meeting with the Father, Son, and Spirit of God, there was great confidence in their law of pure love. This love is sometimes called agape love because it is divine love. It is higher than just human love. Agape love *gives*, while human love tries to *take*.

"Should anyone choose to disobey God, We had a plan that would eventually conquer evil, should evil arise. Grace was and is Our plan.

"After some time, the war in heaven came to a stop. The Father sent Lucifer and one third of the angels to the earth. The new world. Our new creation.

"We had created the earth in six days and rested on the seventh to signify Our day of rest forever. We created man and woman—Adam and Eve—in Our own image.

"Because We chose to create angels, then later on human beings, with power of choice, We ran a great risk. But because of Our plan of salvation, We knew that eventually pure love would conquer evil. So We created earth in six days. Our greatest creation was the human race. We created man and woman in the 'image of God' (Gen. 1:27). Human beings were created with the power of choice to love God or disobey Him.

"After I formed them from the dust of the earth and breathed the breath of life into their nostrils, I had perfect friendship with them. Every evening I joined them on earth, exploring the trees and flowers and petting the animals who were all tame and safe to touch. There was no fear in the Garden of Eden.

"We walked and talked and shared our love. I gave them authority to rule over the whole earth (Gen. 1:28). They were warned about Lucifer, whose name became Satan, the devil. Oh yes, he would test them some day.

"Also, Adam and Eve were given free reign on the earth to eat from all the trees except one. That seems easy, doesn't it? It was a tree designed to test the human race. Would they choose to be loyal to God? Or would the devil be more attractive to them?

"Sadly, one day, Eve wandered from her husband. As she did, she looked at the forbidden tree and heard a voice. She looked closer. All the angels of heaven must have wanted to shout: "Don't go near that tree, Eve!" But it was her choice. Eve drew closer to the voice and spotted a serpent, a snake, talking to her. He was eating a piece of fruit—some say it was an apple—and he offered her a bite. At first she refused, but he delighted her with the thought that she would be as a 'god' if she ate. She was enticed, so she ate."

"For the wages of sin is death; but the gift of God is eternal life through Jesus Christ our Lord" (Rom. 6:23).

To be continued ...

The Longest Journey
Part 2

"In a short time, Eve took some of the fruit to Adam, her husband. When he discovered the fate that was upon her, he reached out and deliberately ate some, too, not wanting to lose her. For God had warned them both that they should die if they ate of it. At that moment, Satan became the prince of this earth, and evil was here to stay until the plan of redemption could be fulfilled.

"The devil is the prince of this world now. He's the ruler. Adam gave it to him. And God allowed it because He said the universe will be established in *freedom*.

"The only temptation on earth, not to eat of the fruit from the tree of knowledge of good and evil was the beginning of sin. And the longest journey began for Me as I became the Savior of humanity at the moment sin began. God promised I would die in their place. Genesis 3:15 tells about the plan of salvation that was set up in heaven in that great committee meeting should sin come to earth.

"I hang here, suffering not because of nails, thorns, spit, mocking, or verbal abuse, but suffering because My Father had to turn His face from Me so I could follow through with the only plan that would save humanity.

"Looking back, I remember how Adam and Eve were sent from their beautiful home—the Garden of Eden. I remember their first two children, faithful Abel who was killed by his brother Cain. Then, when Seth was born, Adam and Eve had much joy. Indeed humanity spun out from Seth, the third son of Adam and Eve. They hoped Seth would be the Redeemer. Every Jewish home after that hoped their firstborn son would be the Savior, the Messiah.

"God had warned Adam and Eve they would die if they gave into the temptation to eat of the forbidden tree, but they did not die right away. They died after a long life, and they are sleeping in the ground awaiting My return when I will wake up those who died in Me. But that's getting ahead of the story. Adam lived 930 years. That's a long time to think about your sin.

"This evil, started by Adam and Eve's bad choice, has corrupted every human system and civilization with progressive evil. Lucifer became the devil. Satan is the prince of this planet with power to rule until the full plan of salvation is accomplished. All people are sinners. All now have a Savior, the Messiah. Yes, here I am, hanging on this cross. All people have a right to choose God and His law of love, or not. That's choice in its perfection.

"Adam's family was not so good. Adam and Eve sinned the first sin, but as their children, grandchildren, and great-grandchildren grew up, sin duplicated itself. I was so sorry to see this blatant sin. Especially since I looked over the face of the earth, and I could find only one man who was on My side. Noah.

"I gave this great man a new commission to Build an ark. There had been no rain yet, so I had to lay out the instructions for building a large boat that would float above the world of water. He obeyed and saved his life, and his family, the animals, and birds, too. In fact, he had a floating zoo. After 150 days, the waters receded, and they were free to populate and explore the world once again.

"What a mess. What was once perfect earth now looked jagged; the beautiful gems on top of the earth were swished under the earth. Mountains rose high, oceans were now too deep to swim in. Many of the animals became wild. The earth had to be replanted, restored, and repopulated.

"God had been careful to give Noah a promise. He set His bow in the heavens— the beautiful rainbow as a sign of His promise, a promise to never destroy the earth by flood a second time.

"Many people grew fearful of God, not trusting Him, and they started to build a tower to heaven so they would never drown. What folly. God stopped the work by giving the people diverse languages at the same time. Now people divided into groups as they found others with the same language.

"As I am thinking about that great flood, I am reminded about the fire that will one day surround the earth. But that's getting ahead of My journey.

"People spread out all over the earth. People forgot God. However, there was another man who was faithful to His Lord. Abraham served God, worshipped Him, and obeyed Him. Christians, Jews, and Muslims regard Abraham as a common ancestor. They all believe in One God who is the creator of everything.

"God handpicked him to be His servant, the father and leader of His people. The miracle of Abraham's child in his old age was one of Our delights. Abraham, 100 years old, and Sarah, his wife, 90 years of age, smiled down at Isaac, their child. They played with their promised boy as if new life had come into their bones. I take much pleasure in remembering this faithful family.

"He that believeth and is baptized shall be saved" (Mark 16:16).

To be continued …

The Longest Journey

Part 3

"From Isaac came twin sons, Jacob and Esau. As so often happened in those days, one boy chose God, one ran from Him. Jacob became the chosen father of twelve sons who in time became the tribes of Israel. Thus began the history of the Jewish nation.

"Talk about a journey. My people in Israel were thrust out of their promised country many times. Jerusalem, the capitol of their country, was My great joy. And yet, as idolatry (serving gods other than the true God) set in, My sadness over Jerusalem knew no end.

"In fact, just the other day, the first 'Palm Sunday,' I cried publicly over Jerusalem. The people wanted to make Me king, but I saw into the hearts of the people and wept bitterly.

"Then I think back to when the Jewish people went to Egypt for 400 years. A famine in the Promised Land drove Israel to Egypt for food. Joseph, faithful son of Jacob, was the hero in those days. Yes, I smile when I think of Joseph.

"Moses, the great leader of Old Testament times, led My children through a forty-year journey on to Canaan.

"Later on, when Israel began building its own community in Canaan, the land God promised Abraham, there were prophets and priests who guided God's people in the way of the Lord. Eager to become like other nations, Israel insisted on a king. This displeased the Lord, who had been their King from the beginning, but He gave them an earthly king.

"I remember the first king. Saul was tall, good looking, intelligent, and he served the Lord at first. But he fell rapidly into sin, finally killing himself in disgrace in a battle. So sad.

"David, the second king, was a man after My own heart. He was author of the psalms and a musician. He won victory after victory in battles for the Lord. He sang such sweet songs of his love for God.

"After David died, many kings followed him. Some did good in the eyes of the Lord, some did evil—sort of a back-and-forth existence for the children of God. Exile to Babylon was the result. Talk about a long journey.

"As I hang here, I remember the prophets such as Isaiah, Jeremiah, Daniel, Micah, Zechariah, and many more. Oh, how they prayed for and preached to the children of God. But the people wouldn't listen. What a tragedy!

"When the world became so tainted with sin that there seemed to be no hope, I, Jesus Christ, the Messiah and Savior of the world was born of the Virgin Mary in a manger in Bethlehem as the Scriptures predicted. This happened at the exact time and place My birth was prophesied.

"Immediately after I was born, Herod issued a decree to kill all baby boys, and in a dream from an angel, Joseph, My earthly father, followed the angel's directions exactly and took My mother Mary and myself and fled to Egypt. Staying there until the angel gave the signal to travel back safely, we took a route to the north of Israel, up to Galilee, to the small town of Nazareth.

"We lived quietly there until I was twelve years of age. Once again we journeyed, this time to Jerusalem for the Passover. Watching the priest kill the lamb, I realized that the lamb represented Me—the Lamb of God—the One meant to be sacrificed for all sin. Then we quietly returned to Nazareth.

"And now, here I am—the sacrifice for all sins of all people. Hanging in terrible agony. Must I hang here alone? Oh yes, that is the plan—the plan of redemption, the plan of salvation. These people before Me are shouting at Me, mocking Me, 'If You are the Son of God, come down and save Yourself.' Oh, Father, I either save Myself, which would be easy to do, or I continue on the cross—the hardest part of My journey. But I love them all so much. This is called grace, something they don't understand yet.

"I stay on the cross to save all those who will accept My free gift of eternal life. Oh, God, the pain of separation from You is too much. 'It is finished.' Evil has run its course.

"Here is the patience of the saints: here are they that keep the commandments of God, and the faith of Jesus" (Rev. 14:12).

To be continued ...

The Longest Journey
Part 4

"My journey didn't end on the cross. Friday evening was supremely sad for My followers, the angels, and My mother, Mary. Sabbath we all rested. I in My grave, and the Jews worshipping in the temple as usual. But My followers were hiding in fear of the Jewish leaders.

"On Sunday the highest glory shone on Me as I rose from the tomb. I had victory over sin, Satan, and death itself. I, the second Adam, won the prized victory on the cross, but no tomb could hold Me, the Son of God, the Messiah, the Savior of the entire world. What great joy in heaven. And finally what great joy on earth. The followers of God told the story again and again, preaching, teaching, and living as examples of the joy of salvation.

"My next journey was a trip back home to heaven. I returned as a victor. I was no longer held hostage by three ugly nails to a slivery wooden cross. Released from the tomb in a glorious resurrection and risen to glory,I returned to heaven to live in angelic adoration.

"Now, from heaven, I rejoice as My followers accept Me, but I grow sad when others reject Me as their Savior and King.

"My disciple Peter wrote, 'Salvation is found in no one else, for there is no other name under heaven given to men by which we must be saved' (Acts 4:12, NIV).

"The apostle Paul also wrote, 'For there is one God and one mediator between

God and men, the man Christ Jesus' (1 Tim. 2:5, NIV).

"Many Jews accept Me as Savior, and many more reject Me, saying they have yet to see the promised Messiah. They are missing the reality of a crucified and risen Savior. How I long for them to turn to Me and see My journey for what it is.

"My long journey is not yet over. After watching so many of My people leave home, country, and family because of war, greed, strife, and misunderstandings, My heart aches for My people. The ones who simply choose Me. I think of the Huguenots, the early Christian pioneers, the reformers,the mothers and fathers, the children, the teens who pray so earnestly for family and friends to find their Savior, Jesus Christ, the Messiah.

"Now, I know in human terms the word 'soon' seems as if it should be within the hour; however, humans want things immediately. But I *will* return. It will be the next part of My journey—My journey back to earth to receive My people and take them home to live with Me in heaven for a thousand years.

"Yes, in the future, there will be the promised worldwide fire that will burn up all sin and all sinners, and once the fire is burned up, the smoke will ascend forever and ever. But sin and sinners will not be burning in excruciating flames. No! God is too good for that. He will burn up sin and sinners. The fire will be quenched once sin is no longer. The smoke will arise into the atmosphere, never to taunt the earth again.

"Then I will bring My people back to this earth. I'll touch My foot on the mountain, and the earth will be recreated as before. Adam and Eve, having been resurrected with all of their children, grandchildren,great-grandchildren, and on and on throughout the ages, will descend from heaven to the newly recreated earth, a world of the greatest pleasure I can think of for them, and I will live with them and be their King forever. Paradise will be regained. This is the story of My journey, the longest journey.

Signed, Jesus Christ, your Brother

My Mom's Belief in God

I can still picture Mom kneeling on the kitchen floor, scrubbing and singing, "For I know whom I have believed, and am persuaded that He is able to keep that which I've committed unto Him against that day" (2 Tim. 1:12).

Mom had been raised in an alcoholic family where it was popular to attend church on Sunday morning, even though their heads were aching. Perhaps God could get through those foggy brains. There was always the hope for a better life, but they did not quite reach it.

A few years after Mom married Dad, she started going to a new church that taught messages from the Scriptures that led her to study the Bible for herself. By and by, she was baptized, and the Lord gave her strength to learn to accept life on life's terms with a clear head.

As there were maids to clean her childhood home, Mom had not been taught the more "practical" lessons about how to keep things clean. In fact, before she married Dad, she had never so much as made her bed, washed a dish, or even dusted.

Fortunately, she was a gifted seamstress. Any kind of sewing, crocheting, knitting, or needlework was her domain. She made all my dresses and knitted all our sweaters. She was a very gifted lady.

As I used to watch Mom on her tender knees, scrubbing and singing, I realized how much strength in the Lord she had. She was looking beyond the mundane to a "soon coming Lord."

She also raised dahlias in the backyard. As we lived in San Diego, we always had a glorious crop of those beautiful flowers. She planted each bulb by hand (kneeling once more), and she tended each plant every day, all summer long.

On Thursday and Saturday nights she would arrange the flowers in the twelve baskets we owned. Then she would drive me to the restaurants all over town.

No one said "no" to me. At that time, my dimples were as cute as the flowers were beautiful. My pleading eyes were irresistible. We sold those flowers for 25 cents a basket, returning the next week to replace the old flowers with new ones. We sold those colorful flowers all summer.

When Mom joined her new church, there was a church school connected to the church. In that school they taught the Bible, as well as Christian standards. She wanted her little girl to get a religious education. Those dahlias paid for my Christian education grades one through nine. What a blessing!

One day in the second grade my teacher taught us about the plan of salvation— Jesus died on the cross for ME, this little girl sitting against the wall in the third row. I quickly caught on to the fact that there was "Someone" to believe in, and that was my Jesus who died on the cross for me.

Raising dahlias is not so remarkable in itself, but knowing this one fact about my mom is: when she was 17 years old, she fell in a basketball game and cracked her tailbone. She was in pain all along, and *never* complained.

All our moms are remarkable for something. I praise God for such a dedicated mom.

After ministering in the prison system, I especially think of those mothers who are inmates. Someday, I hope they will find a special way to be the best mom their kids could have.

Proverbs 31:28 says, "Her children arise up, and call her blessed."

My Dad and His Dad

As I handed my report card to Dad, I looked down at the floor and wondered what punishment I would receive.

Then I looked back up into his eyes as he followed the grades down then up, stopping at the F. His eyes slowly traced the line to the word Algebra. He was quiet for a bit. Shame and fear of punishment traveled through my body. I really had it coming, and I knew I did. Not only did I not study hard on my one difficult subject but I just plain did not get it.

After a long breath, my dad reached out his arms and gave me a wonderful hug. He held me long enough to say, "Honey, math has always been hard for you. Next year, after dinner, we will study algebra together."

That was it.

Instead of punishment, I received unconditional love from a man who was already overworked. He didn't need to waste time on a kid who didn't even try. But he loved me, and I felt his special love that day.

When I came home with my report cards, I usually handed them to Mom. I had a lot of C's and D's, but never before an F. And this was my freshmen year in high school. This grade really mattered to my future.

Mom usually had some punishment and a long lecture, but that didn't help me with math. Why I chose to allow it to be so hard, I do not know. But kids will be kids, and I was no exception.

Just the year before in eighth grade, I barely passed my arithmetic class with a D minus. I remember how humiliated I was for such a low grade, yet how excited that I had passed. But this F was my first, and it really scared me. For the first time I felt the depths of failure. However, in some way, that failure goaded me on to try harder after that. And I did, with good results.

After eighth grade graduation the year before, my dad's dad, Grandpa John, tutored me on the eighth grade arithmetic book. He knew my weakness. It was a lovely summer, and I was allowed to ride my bike to his house. We would study for an hour and eat lunch together. I would then bike the five miles home. Looking back, it was a great summer for me—for all of us.

My Grandpa John was a principal/teacher, a very scholarly man, yet he took time out of a quiet summer vacation to teach a little girl who was constantly saying, "I don't get it." Yes, math was hard for me, and I seemed to have an aversion to getting it, or even trying. Yet here was this brilliant gentleman, my Grandpa John, giving me an hour of his quality time every day, all summer.

Shortly after my freshmen year, we moved from San Diego to a small town in northern California. My dad said, "Now, Joy, you are in a new place; you have a chance to 'start again.' I will help you with your algebra, as well as your geometry. This will be our project for one school year."

To his credit, and a lot of "trying" on my part, I received a B in both those math classes. I'll always thank my dad and grandpa for giving a little girl a chance to make it through the hardest part of her early education.

My grades came up my sophomore year, and when I was a junior, I handed Mom my report card. As she looked up and down my grades, she asked, "What happened?" I had straight A's. All I could answer was, "I finally figured out how to study."

I'm hoping that any dad who reads this can see the love that was poured all over me when I was young. Just that little nudge got me through high school, college, and on through my master's degree in music, the subject of my choice.

Many times I've thought of the generosity of these two men in my young life. Two busy men who gave time and encouragement to me just when I needed it most.

The Golden Rule of Matthew 7:12 was their motto: "Therefore all things whatsoever ye would that men should do to you, do ye even so to them."

Overcomers and the Victorious

Joy is my name. I live a joyful life. I know God has given me an incredible life. Romans 8:28 says, "And we know that all things work together for good to them that love God." This is my motto. When I receive criticism from others, it is usually because I'm full of joy even in the midst of disaster.

Well, that joy isn't fake. It's real. That's why I can write with delight. I may not have all the answers, but I've been a piano teacher for fifty years, and I think I have heard about everything that can possibly "hurt" anyone. We talk about it, and the "pain" starts to heal. I'm the first to agree that there's always more to deal with.

As I write *Peace in Prison*, it truly is with much delight. Yes, I'm aware of feelings, tears, anger, and some pretty heavy emotions within other people that really touch my heart, but I have a God who has given me His joy, His strength, His power to change things. Inside my innermost parts I have joy that keeps turning my life right side up, sort of like a gyrostabilizer in a ship.

No one I know, including myself, has come from a 100 percent functional home.

Many of us have been beaten beyond reason, yelled at, ignored, and much, much more in our childhood, thus destroying parts of our early adulthood. The damage can go even into old age if we don't find a way to let God change our thought process and even our destiny.

There is a heaven to win and a hell to shun. God Himself holds out His hand to us and says, "Yes, you have sinned, but there is a way out of sin. Overcoming victory is God's strength given to us in pure love. For God is love. Ultimately, He has an eternal home for us.

Revelation, the last book in the Bible, is full of texts telling about those who will finally be in heaven. And two words stand out as "heaven-bound" people—overcomers and victorious (Rev. 2:7, 17, 26; 3:5, 12, 21; 21:7).

We have to have some thing to overcome; we have to have had some kind of battle to have "victory" over. Sin and its originator, the devil, is the enemy. But God has a way out for all of us.

In the Old Testament Scriptures, God told Joshua to go to battle for Him. Then He said, "Be strong and of a good courage; be not afraid, neither be thou dismayed: for the Lord thy God is with thee whithersoever thou goest" (Josh. 1:9). God wants us to face the problem ourselves, in His strength and power, so we can have our own victory in this battle of life. James 4:8 says, "Come near to God and he will come near to you" (NIV). The battle truly belongs to God. He is the mighty and perfect warrior.

Many people are dealing with a very bad temper. Yet the Bible says, "Be ye angry, and sin not" (Eph. 4:26). Anger is a God-given emotion that has great value once it is under the control of God. Then anger becomes energy for good.

There is no victory without forgiveness. And forgiveness is a process. Forgiveness releases positive energy. Unforgiveness is toxic. Lack of forgiveness is sin. Forgive God, forgive others, and forgive yourself. To forgive is to let it go. Like layers of onions, we can peel away the results of emotional, spiritual, verbal, and physical abuse by accepting God's love, which is the key to all victorious Christianity. Press through to that victory. Once you have received that victory, invite God to fill the vacancy in your soul.

Christian people are not perfect—they are forgiven people. Philippians 1:6 states: "Being confident of this very thing, that he which hath begun a good work in you will perform it until the day of Jesus Christ." No, you will not be "perfect" immediately, but if you accept Jesus as your Savior, you'll find that Jesus has enough perfection to go around for each of us. It is His perfection that counts. Give God a chance.

Be open to God; allow Him to love you without condition. Then you will learn to love others unconditionally, also.

Trust God. I once had an experience that involved major trust in God. Several years ago, I got out of a really bad marriage. That took a lot of courage for me, and it drained a lot of energy from me. Then my mom had a stoke, and my dad and I had to put her in the nursing home per doctor's orders. Soon after, Dad started bleeding.

After some tests, we found out he had cancer of the bladder. I was devastated to be losing both parents, and I suffered from a great deal of emotional pain.

At my lowest point, I decided to trust God no matter what each day provided for my parents or myself. That's when people started telling me that I "shone." That was the joy of the Lord shinning through difficult times.

Dad and I hired a lawyer to help us with Mom's nursing home bills and their property. Dad and I did our best, but as I was either in the nursing home with Mom or taking Dad to one of his nine surgeries, fourteen months of chemotherapy, thirty-six radiation treatments, many emergency moments, and regular doctor's visits, I simply got further behind with the paperwork that was pilling up.

On December 31 the lawyer called and told me he had to have a certain envelope within fifteen minutes, or it would cost our family lots of money. I hung up the phone and looked at my table. It was a very large table heaped high with envelopes. Nothing was filed, sorted, or even understood.

I stood before that huge table and prayed, "God, You know where that envelope is. We need it. Thank You for finding it for me." For once I didn't tell Him how to answer my prayer; I just gave the problem to Him.

After saying amen, I reached my hand deep into the middle of the pile and grabbed the first envelop I placed my hand on—it was the very envelope the lawyer wanted. Looking up to the ceiling, I asked, "How did You do it?" Getting into my car, I trembled with the knowledge that God was right there in the middle of my muddle. Yes, He's there in the middle of all our muddles, sins, crimes, conflicts, sorrows, or tears, and even our joys. *God is there!*

I'm certain that's the moment of my life I finally knew God wanted to be our solution. He wants to be involved in our victories. The battle is not ours; we don't have to tell Him how to run things. We can relax and let Him run our lives. He knows how. When we get in His way, we always botch it up. I no longer tell God my problem and then have the audacity to say, "And here's how to solve it. Please help me." His answers will always surprise us. His apparent "no" is usually, "I have a better solution, just wait a bit."

Romans 8:31 assures us that "if God be for us, who can be against us?" God can overcome every personal battle for us. God's victory is everlasting victory.

Pain and a Promise

Pain is a strange thing. Each of us has pain. It comes in different forms and different degrees.

When my dad was suffering severe physical pain at the end of his life, I did a mental inventory and realized that most of my pain has been emotional pain.

Physical, emotional, or spiritual pain is real. It is also personal. A cut that is bleeding is visible. Pain inside the body may not be so easy to detect. CAT scans, X-rays, and many machines that look inside the body are helpful for finding the source of the pain. But the pain is real, and an individual must have relief.

Emotional pain is often elusive and laughed about, but counselors are finding out that the mind and the heart are very complex to deal with. Self-help books often give people direction for the inner pain.

Spiritual pain seems to be the most complex of all. The conscience pricks at us when we do wrong. Some of us have very sensitive consciences. Other people have pushed away the "still small voice" for so long that the conscience is seared. The results of a seared conscience give the ability to do wrong and not feel bad about it.

Yet, there is a nagging voice to do wrong, and with the person's consent and cooperation, the devil wins, and evil is locked in. Yet, while we struggle to be free of sin, God is there. However, God can and will finally leave a person alone if he or she determines to live an evil life.

Yet, most of us fight the struggle against evil every day. It seems, like Paul of the New Testament, that the good we would do, we don't really do like we plan, and the evil we would avoid, we fall into the trap. Often, it seems that a lifetime of trying and failing appears to be unsuccessful.

There is a promise from God that can pull us out of the mud of wrong living. Jesus left us with His promise, "Lo, I am with you always" (Matt. 28:20). That's a promise of the presence of God, no matter where you are. God created us, Jesus died for our sins, and the most wonderful promise is His presence in our lives every moment—every breath we take, He is there.

The final triumph of God's great promise is Jesus' second coming. No matter where you are or what you have done, Jesus plans to return to earth in the near future and take His followers home to heaven where there will no longer be pain. Give Him the pain you suffer from now. Let go of your pain, and let God heal you. That is His plan if you will let Him.

Grace! Why?

Thousands and thousands of angels adored and worshipped the Son of God. He was held with the greatest respect ever known. Choirs sang unbelievably beautiful music for Him. All heaven delighted in their Ruler. The setting was perfect.

Then one day a black spot called evil entered heaven and ruined the perfect serenity, perfect beauty, and perfect communion between Creator and created angels. Sorrow has never ceased since that ugly moment.

Lucifer, the angel of light, the choir director, was inflamed with jealousy of his own Creator. Pride and vainglory took over an angel who had the highest position in heaven. Pride and jealousy consumed him. After awhile he convinced one third of the angels that he should be in charge.

Then after Adam and Eve were created, Satan set out on a mission to cause them to fall too. His wily deception fooled Eve into eating fruit that God had warned was off limits. Eve in turn offered the fruit to Adam, and he disobeyed God's orders.. When God came to visit the couple in their garden home, they hid from Him out of shame and fear.

My spine tingled when, as a child, I was caught doing something I was not supposed to do. In a small way, I know how Adam must have felt just then.

But here's where grace comes in. Genesis 3:15 gives the promise of a Savior to come and die in their place. God could have zapped out this world, but the Son of God stepped in and said, "I will die for their sin." That's grace.

Many years later, the Son of God stepped down from His adoring angels, became an embryo, was born, showed His created beings how to live, and finally died on a cruel cross for each of our sins. That's grace. And why? The answer is *love*—God's love for YOU.

Pray, for What?

The many times I've been in a jam and sort of prayed myself out of it have been staggering. As a child my prayers were short. Mostly, "Help me, God." In my teens I talked to God a lot about this boyfriend, then another one, always wondering who God had for me as a husband, which at that time, was my only real desire.

As I got into college and found some subjects too hard, I prayed for good grades with an urgency I hadn't known before. God came through, but I also did my part—I studied.

Later on, in a marriage that was complicated and challenging beyond my ability to cope, I found God to be a Friend to just talk with. At that time, God became my constant Companion. Divorce was preceded with lots of time on my knees. Before I took the step into divorce, God sent me an article that changed my prayer life forever.

I don't remember the magazine. I could not even quote it perfectly, but it made a lasting impression in my prayer life. There was a man living in California who was having trouble knowing how to pray. After many attempts he came to the conclusion to pray for the presence of God in his life.

Of course, asking for the presence of God in my life could be the essence of prayer! Why not? I've thought a lot about this prayer. So, I now ask for His presence on a daily basis. To know God is present in my life because I invited Him in is to me the epitome of human experience.

However, many things nagged at me along the way. And sometimes I lost track of my commitment to this prayer. In time, it would get me into more troubles than I could handle. And new things cropped up their ugly heads to deal with. Looking squarely in the mirror one morning, I just said, "Joy, there are many problems you are not dealing with successfully." Then I lifted my eyes toward heaven and asked God for more help in my prayer life.

A few days later a friend talked to me about her "God can." I laughed, and she went on, "I can't; God can." So now I write my troubles out and throw them in my "God can." It works.

The complications of life are a constant battle each day. What we cannot handle, God really can. So now, with His presence and His help with the things I ask Him for, I truly have a good life. One more thing: "help" is a complete prayer. And "thanks" is, too.

Thanks, for What?

After 75 years of living and observing life, it's exciting to think about Thanksgiving celebrations through the years.

I remember the Thanksgiving after World War II. All my uncles were home from the war, and we had a big gathering with everyone in the family in one place. I was just 15 years old. Having all the family together and each uncle still alive was cause for great celebration. Uncle Harold was the only one decorated with a Purple Heart for his injury, but on that day, he was well and with us once again.

It was wonderful to have all of us together alive and well. To hug, to kiss one another, to tease again, even when Uncle Al tweaked my nose once again—what a Thanksgiving!

Many years later in a different town, I was embarking on a new life. My divorce had left me raw. Most of my family was dead. Some of my close friends were dying. I was living in poverty that only another poor person could understand. Actually I was surviving. I had never missed a meal. My part-time job brought in just enough to pay the bills, but it didn't leave much for anything else. I needed shoes and a warm coat. But I knew that was out of the question. My two-room apartment was adequate for my few belongings, but it was not my first choice. I was used to the finer life, but poverty was poking its ugly head up at me, and I was not taking it well.

Thanksgiving day arrived. As was my custom, I started my day on my knees in prayer. After I talked to the Lord about my needs, the word thanks stuck in my throat. I blurted out, "God, I can't even think of one thing to be thankful for, sorry." The silence after that was nearly embarrassing.

Then I took my hands away from my face and looked at them. My hands were dripping wet with my tears as I sat in self-pity.

As if sunshine entered the room, I finally said, "Thank you, God, for my eyes. A friend of mine is blind. My ears. I have had the privilege of teaching music all my working life. Beethoven was deaf." I was coming to the point of excitement when I remembered a friend who could neither taste nor smell. I could. And thinking of a friend who had no hands, I lifted my eyes to heaven and with gratitude in my heart thanked God, saying, "I can feel, not only with my fingers, but with my heart." What a Thanksgiving that was for me!

"O give thanks unto the Lord; for he is good: for his mercy endureth for ever" (Ps. 136:1).

Hope for the Cheater

There was a man named Jacob who experienced the highs and lows of life. In spite of all his weaknesses, he was a man chosen by God.

Abraham, his grandfather, was given the promise by God that he would have a child who would give birth to a nation (Gen. 15). Years later God honored His promise through the birth of Isaac, his son.

Many years later, Isaac and Rebecca bore twin sons. Both were rascals, each in their own way. However, Esau turned his back on God. Jacob was a schemer, a deceiver, a cheat, yet he kept turning to God. This is the secret for overcoming any sin. Turn to God.

We are first introduced to Jacob's scheming ways in Genesis 25 where it tells the story of Jacob robbing Esau's birthright for a bowl of lentil stew. Imagine that!

Later, Isaac was planning on giving the family blessing to Esau, his favorite son, but Rebecca overheard Isaac's plan, and she and Jacob cooked up a plot for Jacob to receive the blessing before Esau could get back home from hunting venison for his father (Gen. 27).

The scheme worked, but the backlash of that crafty plan resulted in Esau's rage and threat to Jacob's life. Wisely, Jacob ran for his life. His mother gave him directions to the land of her birth. While on the run, he had a great dream of the presence of the Lord and a ladder reaching to heaven, where he exclaimed, "Surely the Lord is in this place; and I knew it not" (Gen. 28:16).

Here he was, a thief, a deceitful man, running for his life, and God gave him this dream of encouragement. Many years into his adult life with two wives, two concubines, and eleven sons, he decided to return home. He was devious and scheming all the years he worked with Laban, his father-in-law (Gen. 30). Now it was time to leave. And now with a large family, huge flocks and herds, he faced the terror of returning to Esau, his cheated and angry brother. Once more, God intervened and blessed (Gen. 31).

On the way to meet Esau, Jacob wrestled with God all night (Gen. 32). God blessed that meeting.

After many years elapsed, Jacob had seventeen years of peace. He watched his sons and grandchildren grow up. God honored this tormented fellow with His presence and showed him His plan.

For us all, from the lowest spot in our lives, we can change in an instant as we look to God and wrestle with Him, and we can ask for His blessing as Jacob did. We have a powerful, loving, forgiving God just as Jacob had.

No matter how low our life is or where we are, there is a time to look up, accept God's blessing of forgiveness, and acknowledge God's presence. Grab on to His hand and swing up to the saving life with God. That time is *now*!

Hope for the Murderer

There was a great persecution in the land. Jesus Christ, the Messiah, had just been crucified, resurrected, and ascended back to heaven. People all over Jerusalem and Israel were flocking to hear about this Jesus who claimed to be the Savior.

The eleven disciples were preaching daily. The huge crowds were astonished how God worked out their salvation on a cruel cross just weeks before.

But the religious leaders were not happy campers at all. They wanted things to stay as they were. This Jesus had upset all they were teaching the Jews. The new Christians were thrown in jail, and worse yet, many were killed.

A follower of Jesus named Stephen was "full of faith and power" (Acts 6:8) and was chosen to be a deacon in the new Christian religion.

Saul, an upright and zealous Pharisee, stood by as Stephen preached a lengthy sermon on the history of Israel leading up to the life and crucifixion of Jesus Christ.

They listened until he looked up into heaven and saw the glory of God. He then spoke words that were nearly his last words: "Behold, I see the heavens opened, and the Son of man standing on the right hand of God" (Acts 7:56).

At this point they laid their coats at Saul's feet and threw stones at Stephen, and Saul was in perfect harmony with this murder.

After Stephen's death, Saul emerged as a great persecutor of the Christian people. He even went so far as to get written permission to travel to Damascus, a town 133 miles north of Jerusalem, to murder, imprison, and in general play havoc with anyone admitting they had become a disciple of Christ.

However, God Himself put a stop to all this nonsense when He confronted Saul. He was nearly at the end of his murderous journey when, "Suddenly there shined round about him a light from heaven" (Acts 9:3). He was so startled, he fell off his horse, and the great light blinded him. A voice asked, "Saul, Saul, why persecutest thou me?" (Acts 9:4). The exciting story of Saul's turnaround and his new name "Paul" is in the ninth chapter of Acts.

After such a dramatic touch on the shoulder by God, Saul, now named Paul, gave his life to God and became a great missionary all over the area, telling others about Jesus.

Traveling by sea and land, he started many churches and wrote fifteen books that are a large part of the New Testament in the Holy Bible. A murderer turned into a man of God.

Yes, it is a miracle, but God wants murderers to turn to Him and see what God can do with their lives.

Hope for the Tongue

Peter always had his foot in his mouth. He was a lot like many of us. He spoke. Then he thought about it. This is a sanguine trait. I know all about it. I, also, am sanguine. It's the nature of the sanguine person to speak, then think.

Have you ever said something that hurt someone? Of course you have. If you're not watching your words, this can happen so quickly. Words spoken cannot be erased. But they can be forgiven.

At the worst time of Jesus' life, one of His very closest friends denied his Lord. Peter refused to recognize and acknowledge Jesus as his Friend. He even swore with his denial: "I know not the man" (Matt. 26:74).

For more than three years, Jesus and Peter, along with Jesus' other disciples, walked, talked, and ate together. But at the trial of Jesus, Peter failed to pass the "tongue test."

How did this man, Peter, go so far as to deny his Lord? Probably, step-by-step he allowed his speech to be too free.

He bragged, "Though I should die with thee, yet I will not deny thee" (Matt. 26:35). That night Peter's mouth let off a volley of profanity as he denied his Lord (Mark 14:71).

Jesus had asked the disciples to pray with Him. But all the disciples had gone to sleep, Peter included. Oh, if only Peter had prayed! But he slept.

At Jesus' trial Peter got into the palace of the high priest and stood around the fire and watched Jesus being tried for something He didn't do. It was at this very trial that Peter's mouth fell out of control. He denied Jesus three times. Jesus had predicted Peter would deny Him, telling Peter the rooster would crow as he denied Him the third time.

And just as Jesus said, the rooster did crow. Peter looked toward Jesus. And Jesus turned and looked full into Peter's eyes. Jesus, at this mock trial leading toward

His crucifixion in a few hours, keenly felt the sting of Peter's denial. Yet as their eyes locked, Jesus looked upon Peter with compassion and forgiveness.

With the deepest pity and sorrow in Jesus' heart and eyes, Peter's heart broke. He rushed out of the hall into utter darkness, into a place of solitude. Ending up in Gethsemane where he had slept as Jesus prayed, Peter knelt and sobbed out his grief. He was a transformed man.

The look of forgiveness in Jesus' eyes was not meant only for Peter. It was for you and me, too. Denying our Lord, swearing, having a dirty mouth, saying cruel words, and much more hurt Jesus, but He looks on us with love. Accept His forgiveness and His power over even our tongues.

Peter, as history and Scriptures tell, went on to be the great "rock" as Jesus once predicted. He was gifted with great faith, spiritual insight, and convincing speech. God worked through him for many years to preach Jesus Christ as the loving, forgiving Savior He is. Saving us from all our sins, and Jesus has promised to return. He has a plan and a place for those who give their lives, and their tongues, to Him.

Hope for the Adulterer

King David was called "a man after God's own heart" (Acts 13:22, NIV). How could this happen to a man who committed adultery with Uriah's wife and then had Uriah killed?

When Jesus, the Messiah, was born years later, He was called the Son of David. Yet, here was a man who committed double sin just to please his sexual desires. How can he also be called "a man after God's own heart"?

No Bible character more fully represents the moral range of human passion than David. The Bible stories of King David are found in 1 and 2 Samuel, starting at 1 Samuel 16.

The major part of the book of Psalms was written by David, a poet, musician, and indeed the greatest king in all of Israel. His life shows that even the closest to God fall into temptation. The general trend of his life was spiritual, yet he fell into adultery and murder.

Can God forgive these crimes, these sins against God? Yes, indeed. Let's look at how David reacted when confronted by the prophet Nathan. The complete story appears in 2 Samuel 11 and 12.

Nathan tells a parable to David, and David's angry reaction to Nathan's parable was, "As the Lord liveth, the man that hath done this shall surely die" (2 Sam. 12:5).

Then Nathan spoke these famous words to David: "Thou art the man" (verse 7). David's heart was broken when he realized his crimes, his sin.

The book of Psalms is full of the troubles of King David; how King Saul pursued him with intent to kill him; and later on his own son chasing him. David's emotions ran from heavenly heights to the lowest earthly depths within his psalms.

Trust and faith in God alone pulled him through. No matter what his problems or emotions, he turned to God as his source for answers, protection, comfort, guidance, and blessing.

Briefly, the secret to David's reunion with God was his humble return, prayer, faith, and trust in God for forgiveness.

In his humble prayer, David asked God: "Have mercy upon me, O God ... blot out my transgressions. Wash me ... and cleanse me ... For I acknowledge my transgressions: and my sin is ever before me.... Purge me ... Create in me a clean heart, O God; and renew a right spirit within me. Cast me not away from thy presence ... Restore unto me the joy of thy salvation" (Ps. 51:1-12).

David lay his sins in God's lap. He accepted God's forgiveness and then got on with his life. It was in the past for him. It was in the past for God. His sin was truly and completely forgiven. The same forgiveness is offered to all sinners. All we have to do is accept it.

Hope for the Prostitute

Did you know there was a prostitute in the genealogy of Jesus Christ? Matthew 1:5 mentions Rahab as the mother of Boaz. Boaz and Ruth were parents of Obed. Jessie, the father of King David, was son of Obed. And Jesus, the Savior, was many generations down the line—a direct line from Rahab the harlot.

Joshua 2 tells of Rahab's story of faith.

The Israelites were about to cross the river Jordan and possess the Promised Land. Joshua sent spies to Jericho. Led by God, they came to Rahab's house, and she invited them in.

The king of Jericho soon got wind of the spies, and he sent out a party of men to locate the spies and capture them. When the king's men came to Rahab's house, she hid the spies and lied, saying they must have gone out the gate. The chase was on, but the spies were safe. Rahab hid the spies on the rooftop in stalks of flax.

The stories of God's mighty power to save had reached the people of Jericho. The deliverance from Egypt, crossing the Red Sea, and their many victories in battle put fear into the hearts of the people of Jericho.

Rahab had listened to these stories with much fear and respect for Israel's God. In fact, all of Jericho feared and trembled. But Rahab alone respected God. Notice how God honored her trust in Him.

After the men of the town left on their search for the spies, she went to the rooftop and talked with them. She made a request of the spies to save her and all her family. The spies pledged their promise to save whoever was in her home.

As her home was in the wall of the town, she cleverly lowered the spies down through a window in her house. A red cord hanging down the wall was the men's escape route.

This same red cord was instrumental in saving Rahab and her family. The men suggested she "bind this line of scarlet thread in the window which thou didst let us down by"(Josh. 2:18).

Soon, Joshua lead the children of Israel over the river Jordan and on to Jericho.

God's plan was first rate in this battle. No fighting. No weapons. He had his people walk around the city of Jericho for six days. On the seventh day they circled the city seven times. On the seventh time around, the priests blew trumpets, the people shouted, and the walls came tumbling down.

But Rahab's home and her family were spared. God respected her faith, and she and her family entered into the family of Israel. She is also listed in the "hall of faith" (Heb. 11:31).

James 2:25 mentions Rahab the harlot as being "justified."

There are two other famous stories in the New Testament that assure us that Jesus cares and can save and forgive a prostitute. True stories of Mary Magdalene (John 8:1-12) and the woman at the well (John 4:1-42), both famous prostitutes, are wonderful stories of how Jesus Christ talked with, forgave, and saved their lives, too.

Hope for the Hopeless Case

A judge over Israel for twenty years, Samson was handpicked to free God's people from their enemies, the Philistines. Before he was even born, God talked to his parents and gave them careful instructions for raising him in a special way.

The full story about Samson can be found in four small chapters in the book of Judges (chapters 13-16).

God's people had once again turned their back on God, worshipping the gods of the heathen nations. Therefore, the Lord delivered them to the Philistines.

For the battles and conflicts between God's chosen people and the heathen nations, God always chose a special person to lead out in the warfare.

In Moses' day, as he was leading God's people from Egypt to the Promised Land, Joshua was the leader in battle.

Many years after Samson's day, David, a shepherd boy, killed the giant Goliath. Yet, he was a mere lad.

As the world's strongest man, Samson unfortunately tampered with evil associations and was weak in resisting the heathen ladies. When he met his wife to be, he commanded his parents, "Get her for me" (Judges 14:2). Later on, Delilah dazzled Samson.

At one point, the lords of the Philistines prodded Delilah into getting Samson's secret for his incredible strength. Samson admitted that if his hair was shaved off he would be weak. In a deep sleep, they shaved off his hair. And sure enough, Samson, the strongest man who ever lived, became Samson, the weak man. His enemies caught him easily, put out his eyes, and for years, "he did grind in the prison house" (Judges 16:21).

After many years, the lords of the Philistines gathered to sacrifice to their heathen god Dagon. Samson was invited to the party, so they could make sport of this weak and very helpless blind man.

His hair had grown back, and Samson requested of God to restore his strength. God honored his prayer. With the strength of his younger years, Samson leaned against the two main pillars and the structure fell, killing everyone inside. Thousands of God's enemies were defeated in just a few moments, and Samson went down with them.

Here is the wonderful fact about Samson. In the New Testament book of Hebrews, Samson was mentioned as a man of faith (Heb. 11:32).

So you see, if you think you are physically strong and have blown your life by being weak in your spiritual choices, God is a God of healing who turns people around and uses strong-willed people for His purposes.

God is a healer, and He can still use you within His will. He can still save your life. Samson was fickle with the Lord and played folly with Delilah. But he discovered that the Lord specializes in hopeless cases.

Hope for the Thief

He was the worst of criminals. In prison for murder and insurrection, he was set free that Friday morning …

The leaders of the nation charged an innocent man and ultimately killed Him that Friday …

Two thieves hung on a cross designed for thieves. Both died …

The Messiah hung in the middle between both thieves. He died.

The Messiah died at three o'clock that Friday. He was buried in Joseph's tomb before the sun set on Friday evening …

In the center of this very dramatic day, Jesus Christ, the Messiah, Savior of the people, was tried and cruelly nailed to a wooden cross.

They whipped Him and jammed a crown of thorns on His head. The mob of religious leaders and others yelled, screamed, and mocked Him for hours that Friday. At last, nailed to the cruel cross, His life was snuffed out. He died of a broken heart.

Thinking about that terrible Friday provides a glimpse of life, death, eternal salvation, and eternal damnation. Jesus, the Savior, was the perfect Son of God, perfect and innocent. Yet in His death He died for the sins of every human on earth. And He died alone.

Barabbas, the truly evil prisoner was released—set free—that day as an exchange for the Messiah's life. He did not die yet. He was free to live and make choices once again. We have no record of a change of attitude in his life. So, ultimately, he died and is sleeping in his grave until the Messiah returns in the clouds of glory to take His people to heaven to receive eternal life from the Life-giver. Barabbas was on death row, but he was released only to die later. And he will die in the fires of hell one day unless he finally accepted Christ as his Savior and Lord.

The two thieves, one on each side of the cross, made decisions that affected their eternal destination. They both died soon after Jesus did, but each had opposite eternal destinations.

For a while both of them jabbed words at Jesus. But one thief had a change of heart. And as he looked into the face of his forgiving Savior, he recognized Jesus to be the Son of God. His heart was broken because of his sin. He looked to Jesus and said to him, "Lord, remember me when thou comest into thy kingdom" (Luke 23:42).

His decision to accept the Lord as His personal Savior assured him of eternal life in heaven. Of all the people in the crowd that day, this thief recognized his Savior as the saving Son of God. His choice assured his eternal life.

Barabbas and the one thief died but will be resurrected when Jesus comes. At that time they will die once more in the flames of hell. In God's mercy, when hellfire covers the entire earth, the wicked will burn up quickly. Also, the land, sea, and air will be cleansed, and sin will never rise again.

Eternal life is the promise to all those choosing and accepting Jesus Christ as Savior. Jesus did His part on the cross; choosing Him as our Lord, Savior, King, and Best Friend is our part.

Both thieves died the first death at that time, but the one on the right hand of Jesus will be resurrected to eternal life when Jesus returns in the clouds of glory. His decision for the Lord at the very end of his earthly life assured him of a place in heaven and in the earth made new.

On that Friday, the saddest day of all history, when Joseph and Nicodemus buried their Lord and Savior, no one knew (or even expected) the surprise that came on the third day.

Early Sunday morning Jesus cast off death forever. After resting on the Sabbath, He was resurrected to new life. Because He died for our sins, we are assured of an opportunity for eternal life. The choice is ours.

The angels in heaven and the followers of their Lord on earth rejoice with glad anticipation for everlasting life.

Yes, there is hope for a thief.

Hope for the Murderer

Sometimes God chooses certain people for specific jobs. In Egypt God picked a family to have a special baby. He was chosen to be the leader of His people, leading them back to the Promised Land.

Jochebed and Amram already had two children, Miriam and Aaron. It was a time of great sadness for God's chosen people. They were actually slaves to a cruel Pharaoh. Then a baby was born with the destiny of leading the children of Israel back to God's country.

But there was a major problem. The Pharaoh pronounced the death sentence on all the baby boys born to the Israelite women. Jochebed kept her baby in her home until he was about three months old. When his cries were too strong and she knew the authorities would kill her baby boy, she devised a plan.

Making a basket and waterproofing it, she carefully cradled her precious "promise boy" in this basket. She knew the place Pharaoh's daughter took her morning baths, so she placed the basket in the river and left Miriam to watch over the basket.

When the princess came for her bath, she heard a baby cry. At once she called for one of her slaves to bring the basket to her. Her heart was touched when she saw the beautiful baby's face. Quickly she decided to adopt this child as her own. She called the baby "Moses" because she drew him out of the water.

Meanwhile, Miriam came to her and declared she could find a good nursemaid for the baby. It was all arranged, and the baby was back in his own home.

So Moses got his first training in a godly home. This early training guided him all his life.

Once he was 12 years of age, he left his home and entered the palace to learn the ways of the kingdom of Egypt. He gained wisdom and became "mighty in words and in deeds" (Acts 7:22).

When he was 40 years old, he remembered he was called of God to deliver God's people. He took a trip into the fields of the workers and found an Egyptian beating a Hebrew slave. Sudden rage drove Moses to kill the Egyptian and hide his body in the sand.

The very next day he went to the field again. But this time, he was met with two Israelites quarreling among themselves. One turned to him with venom in his voice. "Are you thinking of killing me as you killed the Egyptian?" (Exod. 2:14, NIV).

Moses then realized that his actions from the day before had been observed. He knew the palace would soon find out about the murder.

He ran and ran until he came to another country. He attached himself to a family who herded sheep. There he found refuge. He was 40 years old. He married, had children, and watched sheep. He actually lived a very quiet life. We would say he kept a low profile.

Then, when he was 80 years old, God came to him in a fiery bush that did not burn up. At that holy ground, God Himself gave Moses His plan for His chosen people.

After all these years, Moses had forgotten the Egyptian language and was sputtering to God about his inability to speak fluently. Years earlier he had attacked the enemy on his own plan. Now God had a plan that seemed impossible. But he was dealing with the God who turns impossible into possible. The once murderer became the most patient and humble leader of all history.

Leading sheep for forty years was the school designed to teach Moses meekness, patience, and trust in God alone.

The dramatic story in the book of Exodus tells about the ten plagues, the release from slavery for God's people, and the long journey from Egypt to the Promised Land. The story is history in its finest.

Yes, indeed, there is hope for the murderer. God also has a plan for you.

Hope for the Immigrant

She was a girl out of her element. The language and customs that surrounded her were completely opposite to her childhood training. Her country worshipped idols; this new country worshipped the true God in heaven.

Her idols she could see, but this heavenly God was invisible. Yet, she chose to follow her mother-in-law into God's country.

Many years before there was a famine in the Promised Land. Elimelech and Naomi took their young boys to Egypt where there was plenty to eat.

By and by, the boys married girls from this pagan land. One by one, all of the men died, first, Naomi's husband, and then the two brothers. This left a terrible predicament for the ladies. With no men to protect them, they were in a very bad way.

So, with the famine over Naomi concluded it was best to travel back to her home country. Orpah and Ruth, her daughters-in-law, followed her for a long time. Finally, at the crossroads, Naomi turned to the girls and said, "Go back to your families." Orpah chose to return home, but Ruth clung tenaciously to Naomi. She begged her to allow her to go to the Promised Land with her.

"Intreat me not to leave thee … whither thou goest, I will go … thy people shall be my people, and thy God my God," Ruth begged Naomi (Ruth 1:16). So Naomi allowed her to continue on the journey with her.

In those days it was dangerous to travel, dangerous to follow through with her decision. Going to another land, a new culture, and a new language was a huge challenge.

However, Ruth chose to go to Israel with Naomi. It was not easy for the two widows. Naomi was older. Ruth, being capable of working, chose to follow Naomi's suggestion to glean or gather the wheat in a certain man's field.

Ruth did as she was told. Soon she found favor with the owner of the land. He gave her his protection with the other workers. In a short time, the man, Boaz by name, asked her to marry him. She did.

She was accepted in this strange land, in the land of God's chosen people. By accepting Naomi's God, she found new happiness and full acceptance with the people in the village.

In the book of Matthew, chapter one, the ancestors of Jesus Christ are spelled out. In this chapter, Ruth is mentioned as the mother of Obed, grandmother of Jessie, great-grandmother of King David. Ultimately she was in the lineage of Jesus Christ, the Savior. What an honor Ruth was given, all because she chose God's leading.

God has His eye on everyone. Those who choose His way will ultimately have God's watch care here on earth and eternal life in the heavenly home that God is now preparing for us. It's a matter of choice.

Yes, there is hope for the immigrant.

Hope for the Mass Murderer

Manasseh was a wicked king of Judah. He was only 12 years old when he became king. Then he ruled for fifty-five evil years in Jerusalem.

Manasseh, the worst king of Judah, exterminated thousands of Jews in Jerusalem. He even put the prophet Isaiah in a log and had him sawed in two. Some king! Yet he prayed and turned his life around, and God forgave him.

He chose to murder all the "good" people. The Bible graphically states that Manasseh "was an indiscriminate murderer. He drenched Jerusalem with the innocent blood of his victims" (2 Kings 21:16, *The Message*). He even burned his own children in a sacrificial rite.

In his evilness he exterminated many of God's chosen people, including Isaiah, the great prophet. His cruelty knew no bounds. He put the priests and prophets to death just because he wanted his own way. He killed anyone who spoke up for the good. Tradition tells us that Manasseh put the prophet Isaiah in a log and sawed him in two. Hebrews 11:37 uses the expression, "Sawn asunder." Isaiah's only "crime" was to faithfully reprove the sins of the Jewish nation.

However, one day Manasseh prayed, and God got a hold of his heart. Manasseh was turned around, worshipped the Lord, and was received by God as a chosen of God. The Lord had had enough. In 2 Chronicles 33:11 the Assyrians captured Manasseh and carried this great evil king of Judah off to Babylon.

Then in 2 Chronicles 33:12 and 13 we get a glimpse into his conversion from the murderous evil he was committing. "And when he was in affliction, he besought the Lord his God, and humbled himself greatly before the God of his fathers." Manasseh became a truly humble man, deeply regretting his sin, and God forgave his sin.

Yes, there is hope for the mass murderer.

Hope for the Unthankful

In Bible days leprosy was a most dreaded disease. In fact, anyone having leprosy was banned from living with their family and sent to live outside the town with other lepers. They had to cry, "Unclean, unclean," when others came near them. Leviticus and Numbers defined the rules for lepers. They were inflexible.

Luke 17:11-19 tells the complete story about ten lepers who asked Jesus to have mercy on them. He did. He healed every one of them. As they went to the priest, they were healed. "And one of them, when he saw that he was healed, turned back, and with a loud voice glorified God, and fell down on his face at his feet, giving him thanks: and he was a Samaritan" (Luke 17:15, 16).

Jesus' reaction was, "Were there not ten cleansed? but where are the nine?" (verse 17). Jesus had healed them all. He did not reverse His miracle in the nine unthankful men, but I'm sure it hurt Him.

In America there is a natural God-centered holiday. At harvest time, the culmination of the growing season, we have the opportunity to reflect on the blessings from the ground. Yet, even in the cities or any place where there is not a crop to depend upon for survival and financial support, there is much to be thankful for as one reflects on the many blessings God pours out each minute of our lives. Being behind bars seems, and really is difficult, but there are many things to be thankful for.

Give thanks to God, now.

Give thanks to your family, now.

Give thanks to people near you, now.

Life, itself, is precious. However, if you can't reach a thankful part down deep in your heart, just remember, God still continues to give life, sunshine, rain, and blessings to the ungrateful persons as well as to the thankful.

Yes, there is hope for the unthankful. God bless you, indeed

Hope for the Rager

The disciple called the most loved in the Bible was originally a rager. He and his brother James had severe tempers. Yet, once they received the Holy Spirit and allowed Him to control their lives, they became loving witnesses for the Lord, especially John.

When Jesus was naming His disciples, He called James and John the "sons of thunder" (Mark 3:17).

At one time Jesus and His disciples were rejected in a small Samaritan village. Therefore, they had to travel on to another town. John and his brother James, in their rage, suggested that Jesus "command fire to come down from heaven, and consume them" (Luke 9:54).

At the very end of Jesus' life, as He was agonizing in the Garden of Gethsemane, He asked the impulsive Peter to join Him in special prayer. He also asked James and John (the ragers) to be in this close group of three handpicked disciples to "tarry ye here, and watch" (Mark 14:33, 34).

Jesus' closest disciples were ragers, intolerant, vindictive men, yet they all preached Christ and Him crucified, risen, and ascended into heaven. They had witnessed Christ in action, so they could, with authority, share the gospel of Jesus Christ.

Later, as He hung on the cross, Jesus gave His mother, Mary, to John to take home and be cared for (John 19:26, 27). John had, by then, learned the lessons of godly love. The fire in his soul was tamed, and a loving attitude reigned within.

In 1 John 4:7 and 8 we find a brief description of just how much John's attitudes had changed. "Beloved, let us love one another: for love is of God; and every one that loveth is born of God, and knoweth God. He that loveth not knoweth not God; for God is love."

John had been with Jesus, and that made all the difference. He became the beloved disciple.

Any person whose temper is out of control can experience the turnaround that James and John had. The Lord said, "Ask, and ye shall receive, that your joy may be full" (John 16:24).

When John was much older, he was banished to the Isle of Patmos. There he wrote the book of Revelation, a book dictated to him by Jesus Christ. John's life was turned around by the Spirit of God and by his close association with Jesus.

If you also have a problem with rage, cast it at the feet of Jesus. He's the only one who can change your temperament. He created you and wants the very best for you. Yes, indeed, there is hope for the rager.

Two Thieves, Three Crosses

"On a hill far away, stood an old rugged cross, The emblem of suffering and shame." These familiar words are from the old hymn "The Old Rugged Cross" by George Bennard.

The Son of God hung on this cross. The Hebrew nation looked forward to this event with hope. The Christian people look back to the same event with assurance.

The very Son of God hung on the cross and finally died that day for all the sins of every person. However, His cross was not the only cross. There were two other crosses. One on the right and the other on the left side of Him.

Choices. One thief recognized Jesus Christ as his Savior. The other thief ranted and raved, sneering at the Lord. One thief was given a promise of eternal life; the other thief died eternally lost (Matt. 27; Mark 15; Luke 23). Choices.

The Savior was always offering eternal salvation to all who wanted it. The choice belongs to any individual who wants Him. The irony of the offer is that each of us is free to decide our own fate.

At creation we were created to love God. However, in the creation plan, the Father, the Son, and the Holy Spirit chose to create humanity with the power of choice.

"There is a heaven to win, a hell to shun" (*The Signs of the Times*, April 23, 1894). Jesus Christ, who hung on the cross long ago, offers eternal life to all humanity. At His glorious resurrection the following Sunday, the keys to death were won in the terrible struggle against Satan, the enemy of all humankind. Indeed, Satan is the enemy of God Himself. Choices.

It seems that the fierce battle between eternal life and eternal damnation lies within the heart of each one of us. We make the choice. We make the decision to our final destiny. We either choose life or death. The Savior and Satan both want us. But we can't have both. We can run into the arms of the Savior or fall back into the arms of Satan. Choices.

Christ hanging on a cross between two criminals is significant. After all, He came to save sinners. His entire earthly life was to show his compassion and saving grace for all of us, especially the very greatest of sinners. Jesus promised the one thief heaven. The choice is yours. The choice is mine. Now is the time to decide to give your heart to your Savior. Eternal destiny is within your choice. God bless you in your choices.

Lonely Hearts

When you get down to the bottom of the barrel and you find everyone has forsaken you, God is there. And you will find that He is enough. Friends flee, jobs vanish, freedom may no longer be yours, even health can become an incredible challenge. Self-esteem is no longer yours. All sources of support are gone—all that's left is God. Then you realize that's ALL you need.

Try as you might to make resolutions to improve and change your life, make good choices, and walk in a better direction, you end up failing. But at the bottom of it all is power to do right. There is a will that is higher than your own. At some point in your life, you will discover the power that God can give you when you turn your will over to Him and leave self behind.

Reach out for that power now, dear reader. It's available. Read your Bible, and pray every day. Praying to God is simple. Talk to Him silently or out loud. He can read your thoughts. After all, He created your brain. Yet, sometimes there is no quiet place to talk to God out loud, so talk to Him silently.

In your mind, tell God how you feel. He can handle your anger! He's strong enough to handle all your emotions. Ask Him for His will to guide your life. Ask Him for His power over your evil living and His power to do right.

God comes through. Give Him a try—"I have called you friends" (John 15:15).

Prison—A Way Out

Each of us live in our own prison. Each prison has a key. The lock is bold, and so is the key.

Pain of any kind produces its own prison. There is a lock to emotional pain. Physical pain is often only temporary. However, many suffer long and hard physically.

50

Doctors do their best, and sometimes their very worst. But most pains have a solution.

Being in jail or prison is temporary. The pain of prison or jail is at the top of the scale in terms of emotional pain. Even there, it is only temporary.

You, my dear reader, may be facing the electric chair even now as you are reading this book. The fear is overwhelming. Keep reading.

Loss is another prison that some never seem to recover from. But even then, there is a way out. It may be losing the dearest one in death, or to another person. It may be you have lost this person (or persons) through neglect. A word here or there, a fit of anger. Even to killing the one you love best. These pains all have the same KEY—the same way out.

Whether you like to hear it or not, Jesus is "the way, the truth, and the life" (John 14:6). He said it Himself while He was here on earth. He showed us how to live and gave His very life on the cross for the forgiveness of all sin—no matter how heinous—so that we could have a way out. He gave us the way out of ALL prisons.

In a nursing home there are generally two kinds of "old folks," and sometimes not so old. The nasty, rugged, and ragged tongues that cut down everyone in his or her way like a razor blade. Then there are the sweet ones who appreciate the care given to them and relish the times that someone comes and visits them. Yes, two kinds.

In hospitals there are some with only a minor short-term problem. A couple stitches, a bandage, a pat on the back, a smile, and a quick recovery will be the key to overcoming their pain. Still others are at the end of their prison of pain—some with the smile of their Lord radiating from their faces; some with a constant prayer on their lips; some so close to God that as you approach them you feel your own ungodly manners keenly upon your mind.

Yes, for these people their prison lock has already been opened even as they face their own imminent death. Nothing can sever their close relationship with God. Every moment, dealing with excruciating pain and facing death within days or even hours, they glow with the light of God.

In the pods in jail and the cells in prison, there are many people who have found this God—the God with the key and a way out. They also glow with the light of God, knowing that even though their physical bodies are locked up their own spirits are free—free in the Lord who has opened their hearts to the way, the truth, and the life. They are the ones to meet, to get close to, to ask, "What makes you different?"

Scripture is full of the light and love of God—your Creator, your means of escape. Once you have Jesus in your heart, the prison of pain is released, whether in prison, jail, a hospital, nursing home,a bad home, or a difficult job. The key has already unlocked your pain, and the truth sends you on a life of true joy and pure delight no matter where you are.

Accepting God into your heart is so simple. Just say, "Lord, come into my heart. I wish to be free in You."

"If the Son therefore shall make you free, ye shall be free indeed." That's a promise from the Lord in John 8:36.

God is pure love. He gives this love to anyone who asks: "Ask, and ye shall receive, that your joy may be full" (John 16:24).

God's Comfort Zone

We all suffer from a lot of agony in this life. Sometimes physical agony is so intense that we can think of nothing except the pain. Emotional pain is sometimes beyond even the help of good counselors. Spiritual healing is most important if we are to have life in heaven.

We do not always know how to pray. Perhaps we really don't know how to pray at all. But we keep on praying because we want to connect with the only Source of blessing.

Not too long ago, when faced with more physical pain than I thought I could stand, including the ensuing emotional pain that nearly always accompanies physical pain, I resisted the urge to reach for the bottle of pain killers, and instead sat down on my living room chair, got quiet, and as my teenage friends would say, chilled out.

After a bit of quiet, I blurted out, "God, comfort me." After I prayed that simple prayer, I started thinking about Jesus' promise just before He returned to heaven shortly after His crucifixion, death, and resurrection. He said, "And I will pray the Father, and he shall give you another Comforter, that he may abide with you for ever" (John 14:16).

As I reflected on His promise, and before I pushed my thoughts into the moment, I realized I was in God's comfort zone. There was no flash, no physical healing, no surprise; in fact, there was no one moment different from the other moments while I had been sitting there. I felt as if a blanket, or a comforter, had been wrapped around me.

At some point, I realized I *was* comforted. The physical pain was there, but the emotional pain lifted. I had prayed such a simple request, and God honored me with His promised blessing. The comfort came within three minutes. That comfort has never left me. Little by little, the physical pain is subsiding as I have found some very good exercises to help ease my pain. Yet,the emotional pain has disappeared. The intensity of emotions has calmed down to a sizable, manageable life experience.

How God works through these processes, I cannot tell. But I do know we have a Savior who hung on an agonizing cross and suffered the very worst physical pain. He had a way out. After all, He was the Son of God. He could have come down from the cross, and said, "No one is worth this agony." But He stayed on that cross, enduring physical pain none of us will ever experience. He also suffered emotional pain as the crowd mocked and jeered at Him. And the worst of the worst, His spiritual agony was supreme, for the weight of our sins was on His shoulders.

Christ, the sinless One, stayed on that painful cross until He took His last breath. He was in deep agony because He felt separated from His heavenly Father who could not be in the presence of sin. Christ had to bear that agony alone. No, He didn't have to bear that agony. He could have squeaked out. He could have said, "No way!"

What kept Him hanging before a cruel crowd, before the devil and his tricks, and before the angels of heaven who would have taken His place gladly if they could have? You did. He stuck to the plan He and His Father had established before the world was ever created. Before Adam breathed his first breath, the plan was set, and Jesus accepted that plan on the cross.

Why? Why would the Creator so willingly die that Friday afternoon? Because we were created to live forever. There is an eternal life if we will accept the spiritual victory offered to us. No matter how deep we have been in sin, there is a Savior: Jesus Christ, the Messiah.

Why would the Spirit of God comfort me, an ordinary human being? Why does He continue to answer that prayer even though I prayed it only once? Possibly because this one thing was all I really needed. The Comforter is a promised blessing. Pain has a time frame. The promise about pain is in Revelation 21:4: "And God shall wipe away all tears from their eyes; and there shall be no more death, neither sorrow, nor crying, neither shall there be any more pain."

This promise is beyond our short time frame here on earth, which is short at best. That promise is eternal.

I have asked myself many times why God is so willing to follow through with such requests. Pure love is the only answer I can come up with. So, I say, dear reader, reach out. Ask God to comfort you. He is standing there ready to answer that pure prayer, that prayer for the blessing of comfort.

At the Feet of Jesus

Angry men brought a woman to the feet of Jesus. They made her stand in the middle of the crowd at the very feet of Jesus. Their eyes darted vengefully toward her, and their voices challenged the Savior of the world to have her killed.

Men stood ready with large stones ready to snuff her life out. Hatred enveloped the scene, hatred toward Jesus as well as at the woman.

Yes, indeed, she was guilty. They had dragged her right out of an adulterous bed. As she stood at the feet of Jesus, she figured her life was about to end. She knew she had done wrong according to the commandments of God: "Thou shalt not commit adultery" (Exod. 20:14). But she had chosen to give in to her sexual urges, and she sinned against her God. In those days, stoning, not prison was the penalty.

The Jewish leaders were setting up a trap for Jesus, and the trap looked to be airtight. They sneered at Him, "Master, this woman was taken in adultery, in the very act" (John 8:4). According to Jewish law, she had to be stoned to death.

The challenge to Jesus brought an incredible response. He knew the law. He knew if He just forgave her they would say He was against the law of Moses. If He condemned her to die, there would be the Roman officials to contend with. He was truly trapped. But Jesus was the Son of God, and His life of purity, of constant contact with His Father in heaven, would see Him through this test. He saw their scheme, so He stooped down and wrote with His finger on the sand. He said, "He that is without sin among you, let him first cast a stone at her" (verse 7). I'm sure the woman was ready for that first stone. She must have flinched, cowered, and dreaded the torment and final death sentence she had coming.

He continued writing on the dust of the temple floor. The eldest man stepped forward and read, to his surprise, his own sin. He left, guilt ridden. Jesus continued to write. Each man from the oldest to the youngest continued to read what Jesus wrote on the floor of the synagogue. Each one left in silence.

When all the condemning men were gone, Jesus told the woman to look around, asking, "Woman, where are those thine accusers? hath no man condemned thee?" (verse 10). She answered, "No man, Lord" (verse 11).

I feel that this is the way Jesus looks at each of us sinners, for He died for our sins, canceling all our sins if we only ask Him to. Accept Him as your personal Savior, and do just as He told this woman.

He said, "Neither do I condemn thee: go, and sin no more" (verse 11).

What a Savior! What a blessed response to sin!

A Man Called Peter

Peter was with the disciples in a small fishing boat on the Sea of Galilee one evening. Jesus had dismissed them to sail toward the other side of the lake, and He had stayed by to dismiss the 5,000 people who had come to hear Him speak. When they were gone, He walked up the mountain where He so often prayed to His Father in heaven. Then He started on His journey toward the little boat. Walking on water was as natural to Jesus as walking on the earth. By now, the ship was being tossed about by the waves.

The disciples saw something moving on the water and thought it was a spirit. But then Jesus spoke to them and told them not to be afraid. After Peter heard this, he cried out to Jesus, "Lord, if it be thou, bid me come unto thee on the water. And he said, Come" (Matt 14:28, 29). In all his brashness, Peter jumped out of the boat and walked on the water toward Jesus. But the exhilaration was too much for him, and he turned his eyes off Jesus and looked at the waves. At once, having his eyes off the Savior, he started sinking.

"Lord, save me," blurted out Peter (verse 30). God answers prayers appropriately, and always at the right time. He reached down His hand to Peter, lifted him up, and the two of them walked toward the boat together. Peter was indeed humbler after that experience.

So often in the Word of God, we see Jesus' response to people's frailties. Peter had an inappropriate proud and fearful moment. Looking at the threatening waves pulled Peter's gaze away from Jesus, the One who created him, the Savior who would die on the cross for him, and the One who will return to take all those who love Him home with Him. Jesus is planning a home in heaven for us for eternity. This very God answers our plea for help, always just at the right time and in just the right way. And remember, "Help" is a complete prayer, and "Thanks" is a great response, too.

Blinded

God seems to respond so differently to each of us in our trials, temptations, and general life. For Mary, the lovely mother of Jesus, He sent an angel to tell her of the great responsible she would have as the mother of the Savior of the world, but he assured her to "Fear not" (Luke 1:30).

To Adam, He once asked the question, "Where are you?" He knew Adam was hiding because he had just eaten the forbidden fruit.

To Job, He was silent for a long time while Job questioned God about his misery. He had lost his family and his wealth, and he ended up sitting in ashes to help soothe the boils that covered his body from head to toe. Physical, emotional, and financial pain to the max—and God was silent for a long time. Yes, God did finally answer Job's questions, and He remarkably restored his wealth, doubling it and giving him ten more wonderful children. Job lived to play with his great-grandchildren on his lap. He was blessed beyond belief, but what appeared to be God's initial silence nearly overwhelmed Job. However, he remained loyal to God.

Then there was a man named Paul in the New Testament. He was a Jewish Pharisee, and one of the top leaders in Israel. Jesus Christ had recently been crucified and had risen from the dead. He left behind eleven disciples and thousands of believers who were growing in number every day.

Paul, first called Saul, was one of the Jewish leaders who with religious power and zeal pursued the early Christians, killing them, putting them in prison, and in general making havoc for the believers. But one day, God put a stop to his vengeful ways.

Paul (still called Saul at the time) was given a mission to travel to a town far north of Jerusalem, a town called Damascus, to arrest and do away with all the believers of Jesus Christ, the Messiah.

But God intervened. As Paul and his fellow travelers were about to enter the town of Damascus, a bright light blinded Paul. God did not use gentle treatment for this "madman." God had to get his attention. And nothing short of a blinding light would get the attention of such a determined man.

Blinded and lying in the dirt, Saul looked up, and heard, "Saul, Saul, why persecutest thou me? And he said, Who art thou, Lord?" (Acts 9:4, 5). Well, at least he realized it was the voice of God. Giving Saul instructions, God let him stay blind and gave him a humble trip into the very city in which he intended to create havoc. Saul was converted, and his name was changed to Paul. In three days, his sight was restored, and God and Paul had a close connection for the rest of his life.

Sometimes it takes lightening to get our attention. God wants our heart; He wants our entire being. He can use us as instruments to proclaim the goodness of God to the people right around us.

Once surrendered to God, Paul's life was one miracle after another. God commissioned him to take the message about Jesus to the Gentiles, the people outside the Jewish community. The very message he tried to squelch, he proclaimed all over the then-known world. His travels and experiences fill much of the New Testament, starting with the book of Acts. It's exciting to read about how God used him for good. Paul had an incredible life once he got on the right side. We can, too

A Big Fish Story

Skeptics don't believe the big fish story in the Bible, but there is much proof that it happened. There are only four chapters that tell the story of Jonah and the big fish in the book of Jonah in the Bible.

Running away from God got Jonah into a lot of trouble. God had a city He wanted to save, and He handpicked Jonah, a prophet, to go to the wicked city of Nineveh to preach repentance. It was a city 500 miles east of his home. Jonah had heard of the wickedness of the people of the town, and the thought of preaching to those people overwhelmed him. So Jonah decided to run the other way. Bad choice.

He went to a town named Joppa and boarded a ship headed 2,000 miles west in the opposite direction. Once out to sea, he went below deck and took a nap. A storm came up with a fury that left the sailors no choice but to throw the cargo overboard.

When the ship was in danger of going under, they cast lots, throwing dice, to see who was on board that had caused this terrible storm, bringing danger upon all those on board.

The lot fell on Jonah. He was brought up topside and questioned. He had to admit his story. He told the men that the storm was his fault. He was a prophet running away from the commission God had given him.

As he stood before the men, he finally asked them to throw him overboard, saying that the ship would then be safe and the storm would cease. The sailors were reluctant to do this terrible thing, but they finally flung Jonah out into the raging sea.

But God wasn't through with Jonah. He had a special work for him to do. And so He prepared a big fish to swallow the prophet. Jonah sank deep into the sea, then deep into the fish's belly. In the belly of the fish (some think it was a whale, but the Scriptures call it a great fish), Jonah was protected from drowning in the sea. The storm subsided just as Jonah predicted, and the sailors were saved.

The many ways God deals with His people is often amusing. And this is one of the most amusing and amazing stories in the Bible. Jonah stayed in that fish's belly, feeling doomed. No place to go, no one to talk with, nothing to eat, guilt dripping from the pores of his skin. No place on earth could have been more terrible or more terrifying.

While in the belly of the fish, Jonah finally talked to Someone who did hear him. He prayed as never before in his life. And God had the fish throw up Jonah on a seashore near Nineveh. Then God indicated that the commission to talk to the people of Nineveh still held true.

This time Jonah obeyed God's will. Traveling over land until he reached Nineveh, he finally took courage and walked the streets of the city. It took him three days to cover the city. His short message went like this, "Yet forty days, and Nineveh shall be overthrown" (Jonah 3:4).

He didn't whisper the message. He used all the voice he could to shout the message. Then Jonah expected to step back and watch God destroy the city. But the king heard the message, fasted, and prayed to God to forgive him and his people's sins. They all prayed for their lives. They all repented solemnly and sincerely.

When God saw how contrite the people were, He accepted their sorrow for sins and saved the city from utter destruction.

God's reaction to Jonah in the ship, His reaction to the people of Nineveh, and His reaction to all of us when we turn our face toward God is always surprising. God wants His people to be safe in His arms, doing His will. And when anyone is out of the will of God, He seems to take great measures to get our attention and get us on the right road again. This He did for Jonah. This He also did for the whole city of Nineveh. This He will do for you and me, too. What a God!

Forty Years With the Scorpions

God has a work for every one of us. Certain people are picked for small jobs and some for more difficult jobs, but God has a plan for each one of us. And a few are picked out for a special work. Moses of the Old Testament was one very special person God picked out before he was born.

The story appears in the beginning of the book of Exodus, and it is full of unusual, but not accidental, episodes. Moses' birth came at a time when the children of Israel were slaves in Egypt. The Pharaoh had commanded the baby boys of the Israelites to be thrown into the river and drowned. Pharaoh felt that the Israelites were becoming too strong for his country.

Moses' parents were aware that God had handpicked Moses to be the deliverer of God's people. Putting their baby in a basket and floating him on the river, they allowed God to arrange the fate of this special baby. Moses' sister watched as Pharaoh's daughter came to the river for her morning bath.

When she heard a baby cry, it touched her heart, and she asked for the baby to be brought to her. Instead of drowning the baby, she adopted him. Asking Miriam, Moses' sister, to find a wet nurse to care for the baby, she gave the baby back to his own mother. It was understood that at age 12, he was to enter the court of Pharaoh and train to be the next leader of Egypt.

Until he was 40 years of age, he trained in the language of the land, military strategy, history, and all the education a leader must know to lead a country. Pharaoh's daughter was training her adopted son to rule her nation.

Meanwhile, Moses, who had been raised by a God-fearing mother and father, was fully aware that God had His hand on his life.

One day when he was 40 years old, Moses left the courts of learning and walked into the fields to observe the people. His blood ran hot as he saw an Egyptian beating an Israelite. Right there, he killed the Egyptian, buried him, and went back to the palace.

The next day he went to the fields once again. This time two Israelites were quarreling together. As Moses moved toward them, one of them asked, "Are you going to kill me the way you killed that Egyptian?" (Exod. 2:14, *The Message*).

Extreme fear filled Moses when he realized people knew about the murder from the previous day. And without returning to the palace, he fled into the wilderness, to the land of Midian, and stayed there for forty years.

So the story progresses in Moses' life in the wilderness. He came upon a friendly family, married one of the girls, had two boys, and acquired a very wise father-in-law. However, as nice as that all seems, Moses lived the next forty years with his guilt while herding sheep and dealing with the snakes and scorpions of the desert in the land of Midian.

One day Moses came upon a burning bush. As he watched the bush burn, the fire did not consume it. He was drawn toward the bush.

Now, here's where God got the attention of this special man. God spoke to Moses from the burning bush: "Put off thy shoes from off thy feet, for the place whereon thou standest is holy ground" (Exod. 3:15).

God's reaction to Moses' murder forty years earlier was to teach humility to a hot-headed, well-trained military genius and mold him into a mild-mannered, yet strong leader—one that God could work with.

The rest of the story is history. The book of Exodus is an incredible book that depicts God's deliverance of His chosen children and the leadership of one handpicked man.

God has a plan for your life, too. You may feel you are placed on a shelf. And that may be for a time, but on that shelf God has a way of creating within you the ability to do a good work for Him when the time and circumstances fall into place. God's deals with each of us individually and uniquely. Allow Him to lead you and anticipate the surprises He will have in store for you.

The Unpardonable Sin

At one time or another we all ask the question, "Have I committed the unpardonable sin?" Since you are reading this and seeking God, and the answer is no, you have not committed the unpardonable sin.

"Come now, and let us reason together, saith the Lord: though your sins be as scarlet, they shall be as white as snow; though they be red like crimson, they shall be as wool" (Isa. 1:18).

"The closer you come to Jesus, the more faulty you will appear in your own eyes; for your vision will be clearer, and your imperfections will be seen in broad and distinct contrast to His perfect nature. This is evidence that Satan's delusions have lost their power; that the vivifying influence of the Spirit of God is arousing you" (*Steps to Christ*, pp. 64, 65).

"The most common manifestation of the sin against the Holy Spirit is in persistently slighting Heaven's invitation to repent" (*The Desire of Ages*, p. 324).

"When the soul surrenders itself to Christ, a new power takes possession of the new heart. A change is wrought which man can never accomplish for himself. It is a supernatural work" (*The Desire of Ages*, p. 324).

Indeed, Jesus Christ changes our hearts through the Holy Spirit. It is through the "inner voice," the conscience, that the Holy Spirit speaks to us. This "voice" is the essential part of our being that we must not avoid.

We will be impressed to confess our sins, to repent, to turn from sin. This is possible only by the presence of the Holy Spirit in our lives. "If we say that we have no sin, we deceive ourselves, and the truth is not in us. If we confess our sins, he is faithful and just to forgive us our sins, and to cleanse us from all unrighteousness. If we say that we have not sinned, we make him a liar, and his word is not in us" (1 John 1:8-10). Mistakes and flaws are proof we are human.

I remember the time I did something very foolish. My friend Ethel said, "Well then, do as the Chinese do. They say, 'Just do the best you can.'" After awhile, my life was going well again. I still blush over by blunder, yet immediately I feel the cool rush of recovery, not because of some Chinese saying but because I know that Jesus only expects my best, and He loves me unconditionally. I'm certain I'm a better person because of that experience. All of us sin, but we do not have to stay in our sin. Jesus is our Savior, saving us from our sins as we ask Him for victory over sin.

Romans 8:28 tells us, "And we know that all things work together for good to them that love God." I personally choose to hang onto this text for dear life.

Cain, Esau, Pharaoh, King Saul, Jezebel, Ahab, and Judas are people in the Bible who demonstrate how they turned their back on God, living in self-will, rejecting the Holy Spirit again and again until the Holy Spirit left them in their sin.

On the other hand, the Bible is full of people who sinned, repented, and turned from their sins. They have the assurance of eternal life.

King David's great sin and repentance is an example of the kind of sinner God can work with. After he committed adultery with Bathsheba, David had her husband, Uriah, murdered. And for a while, he lived life as if he did nothing wrong. However, Nathan the prophet confronted him saying, "Thou art the man" (2 Sam. 12:7). David fell to his knees and prayed what I call the "sinner's Psalm," which is recorded in Psalm 51.

"Take not thy holy spirit from me" (Ps. 51:11). King David's double sin, adultery and murder, were overwhelming once he faced them as sin. He asked God, "Cast me not away from thy presence" (*Ibid.*).

The sin against the Holy Spirit is the sin of persistent refusal to respond to the invitation to repent. May we always submit to the will of God as Jesus Himself did when He prayed in the Garden of Gethsemane, "Nevertheless not as I will, but as thou wilt" (Matt. 26:39). What a perfect example!

Starting Again, Again

When December arrives we all start thinking about New Year's resolutions. Put simply, resolutions don't work. Promises to "do better" are like ropes of sand. You can't really grab hold of them. The promises to yourself and others are worthless.

But when December rolls around again and you ponder, "How can I make my life better next year?" it's a great time to tune into Someone who can make life work better this time.

When my life isn't working right, I check myself in to God's workshop. He has a thousand ways to get my life on track and give me joy in the process. Joy is the sign that forgiveness has happened.

Receive Jesus Christ as your Savior. Give your mind and heart to Him. He can and will remake you. Better than that, He can do what a New Year's resolution cannot do. He can give you a painless heart transplant. When you pray, "Give me a new heart, Lord," it changes everything.

God will deliver you from your enemy, the devil, because "He delights in you" (see Ps. 18:19). Instead of looking back at our lives and feeling too sinful for a pure God, look forward, ask for and expect the presence of God in your life.

You may have gotten into serious trouble over money, rape, robbery, theft, murder, lying to cover up, or cheating on your partner. No matter what, we have a Savior who died for our sins. Sins of all sizes—big and little.

December is a great month to look beyond the past, because "all have sinned" (Rom. 3:23) and are in need of a Creator who is also our Redeemer. He redeems us and forgives us of our past. It pays to check out the process for this better life, a life of incredible happiness, no matter the circumstances. Here are the ABC's of prayer:

ASK – Ask for forgiveness (Matt. 7:7)

BELIEVE – Believe He forgives you (1 John 1:9)

CLAIM – Claim His promise of forgiveness (Eph. 1:7)

When you have a bad day, return in your mind to the spot where you left God behind. Ask for forgiveness. If you have failed to ask for God's power to be free from sin, return immediately to Him. Reconnect with God. He is always with you. He will turn your life around once again.

There is no sin God cannot heal. God is not about to give up on you. Go ahead. Ask God for power over sin. Right now. Silently. He will hear your heart.

As you come to God by faith, believing that He can and will reorder your life, He does the work. Your part is to believe in Him. Each morning ask for His power over sin so you can be free. When a person is fully emptied of self, the vacuum is filled by the in flowing of the Spirit of God.

Guilt. God's guilt is good. It leads you to repent of your ways and turn you around. Satan's guilt is bad. It drives you from God. It makes you miserable. So check out just who is giving you the guilt. Claim His promise of forgiveness(1 John 1:9).

Find out God's plan for you; then use all of whatever ability He gives you to carry out that plan. His very will is for you to connect to Him and stay connected. Jesus said, "I am the vine, ye are the branches" (John 15:5).

Give your will to God. Then God can control your will, and it will be constant and steady. When you are in connection with Christ, you will gain victory over sin.

Our sinful nature is so strong that it is impossible for us to become free from its control by our own efforts. God requires of us the impossible. But He can do the impossible in us. God assures us that "My grace is sufficient for thee" (2 Cor. 12:9). The power of sin was broken on the cross. Just believe this for yourself.

God can take your bad habits and make your life happy beyond your wildest imagination. Drugs, alcohol, or tobacco are no problem for God. Sure, if you need medical help, get it. God can work through the doctors. He created them, too.

In God's light, we see our own darkness. A few minutes with Him and our darkness disappears. As I've mentioned before, when King David committed adultery with Bathsheba and murdered Uriah, her husband, he turned to God and prayed, "Create in me a clean heart." I can't stress this enough how powerful Psalm 51:9-12 is. It is the perfect prayer when we have sinned again and again.

God gave a promise to Abraham in Genesis 15:1. He said, "I am thy shield and thy exceeding great reward." Just imagine that! God is your greatest reward. The reward to make all other rewards fall into insignificance.

So many people think of heaven as their reward. Actually, God Himself is our reward. Heaven is God's home. And right now as you are reading this, He is preparing a home for you in heaven. No beauty on earth can describe it. No feeling you may have can compare to what awaits those who choose God.

Why not give God a chance to make your life all it can be here and now. Ask, believe, and claim the very best for yourself. He promises to always be with us "even unto the end of the world" (Matt. 28:20).

God bless you as you make God your delight.

Choice, Not Chance

Many games hinge on luck or chance. Indeed even strategy cannot overcome games of chance. "That's the chance you take" is a common comment when you lose.

Casinos are full of people taking a "chance." The jackpot seems to be the only goal in life for many people. And survival of the fittest seems to have a bit of luck tucked away somewhere.

Many people believe that even the introduction of the human race happened by chance millions of years ago. However, the Creator of this earth doesn't work by *chance*. He works by *choice*. And those people who love Him live by choice, not by chance.

Many years ago in a heavenly meeting between God the Father and His beloved Son and the Spirit of God, a choice was made to create the earth.

In the excitement and delight of this plan of creation was a built-in secondary plan, just in case something might go wrong. Sure enough, the bright and shining angel Lucifer, the highest of all angels, developed a serious case of jealousy. He chose to let pride rule his life.

After earth was created, Lucifer declared war with God in a jealous rage. Lucifer then convinced one third of the angels to side with him against the Lord God. God finally had to cast him out of heaven. Falling, falling, falling from heaven, his destiny was this planet, which was the newest creation of all the planets.

The Bible is clear in the early chapters of Genesis as to what happened next. Chance had nothing to do with it. Eve chose to accept the forbidden fruit from

Lucifer, now called Satan or the devil. Adam also made a seriously bad choice. He took the fruit from Eve and ate it.

From that moment on this once beautiful planet was plagued by evil. The Bible is full of the results of evil that the devil has wrought upon earth's inhabitants.

But God had His say in the matter. He already had His plan prepared, and He chose to put that plan into action. Genesis 3:15 states the promise God gave to Adam and Eve: "And I will put enmity between thee and the woman, and between thy seed and her seed; it shall bruise thy head, and thou shalt bruise his heel."

The Lord was talking directly to the devil. He was laying out the plan of redemption before the devil in the presence of Adam and Eve. The promised Savior would chose to "save his people from their sins"(Matt. 1:21).

One dark night in a stable in Bethlehem, in the presence of the animals, a Baby was born. A Baby destined to be our Savior. A Baby conceived by the Holy Ghost. A Baby who would grow up to be the Son of man, a perfect example of how to live.

His choices were not directed by the devil. His choices were pure, even when the choices themselves went against the leaders of the land. He showed us how to live.

Finally, one Friday the leaders of Israel, giving into the pride and jealousy that was inspired by Satan, nailed the Savior to an old rugged cross. The Savior stayed on that cross for six painful hours by choice. There was no chance there. And for a long sad weekend, it looked like Satan had won.

It seemed to the disciples and friends of Jesus that the Savior was dead and gone. His body was taken down from the cross and buried in Joseph's tomb. And the Sabbath hours began on that Friday night—the saddest Sabbath on earth, the saddest day in heaven.

Jesus rested all Sabbath in the tomb. His work was done. The plan of redeeming His people was complete. As at the end of Creation week, the Lord rested on the Sabbath (see Gen. 1 and 2).

Angels had been present at Jesus' birth. Once again, angels were present that glorious Sunday at Jesus' resurrection. Yes, the battle between God and Satan was over. Of course, the great controversy between Christ and Satan will be fully completed at the second coming of Christ.

Jesus was raised to life. His work on earth was finished. He had His quiet rest in the grave on the Sabbath. And finally, on the first day of the week, with great joy in heaven and on earth, Jesus rose from the grave and praises to the King of kings rang all through the courts of heaven and spread throughout the earth.

Indeed, Jesus' birth, life, death, and resurrection were all by *choice*, not by *chance*.

Wist Ye Not?

The termite man sprayed poison under the house. He was careful to measure the amount of poison. The purpose of the poison was to kill *only* termites. He was careful for the safety of the people in the home, as well as for himself.

The business of the termite man was killing termites to save homes from destruction. Poison must be used or homes disintegrate.

At the age of 12, Jesus Christ, the Savior, the Messiah, learned what His business, His life work was to be. His family took Him to Jerusalem for the Passover. At the feast Jesus watched while the high priest plunged the knife into the neck of the sacrificial lamb.

At a young age, Jesus had studied the Old Testament scriptures at His mother's knee. He now realized that the death of this lamb pointed forward to His death.

The Jews believed at that time that the Messiah would "save" them from Roman power. Many people today believe we should be "saved" from social injustice. Yet Jesus clearly understood that His business was to save people from sin. And Jesus' business ultimately brought His life deep into the poison of sin.

While Jesus intently watched the knife end the life of the lamb on the altar, He became aware of His own fate. With an understanding even most adults don't have, He thought, "My own name means 'He shall save His people from their sins.'" For the first time, he realized He was the Son of God.

"I am to be the Lamb of God foretold in Scripture. I am to be killed for the sins of all people. I am Jesus the Savior. I am Christ the Messiah. I have a special work to do." We can only imagine His thoughts.

Now let's turn to another illustration. The dentist probed around in the back of Helen's mouth. She put up a great fuss. Her knuckles were white with tension as she clawed her nails into the arm of the chair. Occasionally her body contorted in pain. And to be honest, she let out a scream or two. But finally the abscessed tooth was removed; she relaxed with relief as the excruciating pain the tooth had caused her began to ease.

The condition of the earth in Jesus' day was just like Helen's abscessed tooth—rotten, rotten with sin.

Sin is a strange thing. All humans since Adam and Eve have sinned. Some have plunged deeply into it, while others try to avoid it but still stumble and fall. Yet, sin, no matter what degree it is, separates us from God, and a depth of loneliness envelopes us. Loneliness drives us to the point of decision. The point of decision always has two directions: right or wrong.

Melvin, the gardener, grew roses in his spacious yard. When the blooming season ceased, Melvin trimmed his bushes until they looked bare. He cut so deeply into the heart of the bush that his neighbors gasped, "Oh, you killed those lovely rose bushes." But Melvin had vision. He understood the necessity of the deep cuts.

Likewise, Jesus understood the necessity of His mission. He understood the need to cut deep into the hearts of the people and call them to repentance and a relationship with Him in order for them to receive the gift of eternal life.

As a 12 year old, Jesus observed all the significance of the Passover and tarried in the temple long after his parents had left the feast. He quizzed the religious scholars. His thirst for wisdom was so straightforward that these teachers of the law of God were fixed on His questions. Mary and the Holy Spirit had taught Jesus well.

His training was pure and holy. His mind had not been contaminated by any religious tradition. Therefore, he was a most unusual Child to converse with.

One can imagine the rabbis rubbing their hands and clucking as they plotted to capture this Child and mold His mind into their own traditional thinking. Fortunately, that was not meant to be.

Meanwhile, Joseph and Mary folded up the tent and, with the caravan, began the journey toward their home in Nazareth. Sharing the spiritual high with others, they fell into a secular mediocrity, and they forgot Jesus.

As they started to set up camp the first night of the journey, Jesus did not answer when they called for Him to help. Mary and Joseph immediately began searching for their Child.

"Have you seen Jesus?" "Have you seen our Son?" "Has Jesus been by here?" "Oh, Jesus, where are You?" Mary and Joseph called and called for their Son, but He was not with the travelers.

When the feast was over, they had assumed Jesus was with them because He was always helping, always obedient, and always near them. However, Jesus was not there. Absorbed in the pleasure of traveling, they had lost Jesus for one day. Little did they know it would take three days to find Him.

Many people today have tasted the loneliness of losing Jesus for a while. In our busy lives, we are often unaware that Jesus is not with us. If we want to find Jesus, we must search. He will at last be found by those who seek Him.

Jesus' parents anguished over their mistake. With heavy hearts the two parents returned to Jerusalem while the caravan traveled north. God had trusted this Child to their protection, and they had made a grave error.

When they arrived at Jerusalem, they frantically called and searched. Meanwhile, Jesus was calmly sitting in the temple talking with the religious leaders. The Child Jesus was sitting in the middle of a very intellectual group of men. Every eye and all attention was focused upon Him. They were all amazed at how profound a mind Jesus had.

Suddenly His parents appeared in the doorway. Joseph and Mary had experienced grief, fear, anguish, sorrow, which was now replaced with astonishment, bewilderment, wonder, and relief.

Mary scolded Him. "Why hast thou thus dealt with us?" (Luke 2:48). Forgetting that it was their neglect that had brought about this problem, she scolded Jesus. And Jesus asked her a question. He had done no wrong. He had just "tarried" in the temple. With no resentment, but with innocent surprise, He replied, "How is it that ye sought me?" (verse 49).

Actually, His parents had left Him behind. Today many people walk off and forget Jesus. The misery of loneliness that follows demands a return to seek and to find Him. In the twenty-first century, He still asks, "How is it that ye sought Me?" This question deserves our best response.

Then Jesus continued, "Wist ye not." In modern language He would have asked, "Don't you know?" And the next seven words became the keynote of His entire life: "I must be about my Father's business" (*Ibid.*).

At this point, Jesus renounced kinship to Joseph and pronounced sonship to God. The first recorded words of Jesus affirmed His deity. His strong, steady voice expressed a new certainty that He was the Messiah. This 12-year-old Child recognized the mystery of His lifework as He observed the killing of the lamb in the temple.

Ultimately His business was teaching, healing, dying on the cross, and gaining victory over death at His resurrection.

Just as the termite man sprayed poison on the wood; the dentist probed his hands into an infected mouth; and the gardener cut deep down into the rose bush, so it was that Jesus, at the age of 12, knew that his "business"—His work on earth—was to plunge Himself into the deepest parts of sin. Jesus Christ thrust His own life into the leprosy of sin yet He received no pollution.

Sin's deadly poison permeated the world, yet Jesus was *not* contaminated. He was our termite man. He was our gardener. He was our dentist. Indeed, He was our doctor. He had no fear of leprosy or contamination of any kind. How can a holy God take hold of a sinful world and not get contaminated? By grace! By Christ's death on the cross, we are thereby vaccinated against the infection of sin.

Though His wisdom had astonished the doctors, yet He meekly subjected himself to His human guardians. As they journeyed home to Nazareth, the three travelers contemplated the mission of the Messiah, His lifework.

Jesus obediently returned home with His parents. And for the next eighteen years, He worked in the carpenter's shop. As Jesus thoughtfully hammered the nails into the wood furniture, He was spiritually preparing for the nails that would one day be driven through His own hands and feet on the cross.

We can give the poison, the infection of our sin to Jesus our Savior. Our "business" is to believe on His name, Jesus Christ, to accept His saving power, and to tell others this good news.

(The full story of Jesus' experience in the temple at Passover is found in Luke 2:41-52).

Salt

"Mingle with the company." Martha's mother gave Martha last-minute instructions just before the guests arrived for a colossal party she had been preparing for weeks. During all these weeks of preparation, Martha had been dreaming of spending the evening in a cozy little alcove with her fiancée, far from the clutter of glasses and the chatter of people invading her romantic notions. "Mingling with the company" was unmistakably not her idea of a great party.

But somehow Martha released her dream and obeyed her mother's wishes. As the party progressed, Martha's original disappointment gradually faded away. A joyful spirit bubbled on her face. The cheerful aura surrounding her slipped out to the company in spite of herself. Not only was the party a monumental triumph for her mother but Martha's inner pleasure was apparent to all the guests. That night she learned the value of surrendering to someone else's plan.

Mingle with the company. Jesus had in mind the same idea while teaching the disciples how to spread the good news throughout the world. As Jesus sat at the foot of a mountain near the Sea of Galilee, the disciples and a crowd of people gathered to hear His greatest sermon, the Sermon on the Mount, which is also known as the Beatitudes (see Matt. 5). The book of Matthew describes a specific formula for true happiness. Jesus said that happiness comes through your reaction to the difficult times in life.

Since all people have trials, Jesus taught that by developing proper attitudes through trials, we will acquire a genuine and lasting joy-filled life that becomes contagious.

If Jesus had been talking today, He may have used the word happy or fortunate. However, the Holy Bible uses the term *blessed*. At the end of His sermon, He suggested sharing the same rewards with others surrounding them. "Let your light so shine" (Matt. 5:16) as you reflect Jesus in your heart. He also said, "Ye are the salt of the earth" (Matt. 5:13).

As Jesus talked, the people looking beyond Him and noticed the grains of useless salt that edged the trail up the mountainside. Jesus always had a knack of speaking to people about common objects in an uncommon manner. Simple salt supplied Jesus with pungent prose.

These Beatitudes can prevent spiritual bewilderment in our own attitudes. Jesus mentions the following types of trials or difficulties through which we may find true happiness.

They are:
- The poor in spirit
- They that mourn
- The meek
- Those who are hungry and thirsty for righteousness
- The merciful
- The pure in heart
- Peacemakers
- Those who are persecuted (Matt. 5:3-10)

Just what are the qualities that make salt so important? A little boy once described salt as the thing that makes mashed potatoes horrid if it isn't there. The taste buds can hardly tolerate certain foods without salt. Just so, certain earthly situations would be intolerable without the "salt" of human compassion, kindness, and gentleness.

The love of God permeates silently within a community just as salt spreads through food. Salt diffuses invisibly. So does real love. Salt preserves, as does gentleness. Good salt is clean, useful, and necessary. Christian love in action is, too. A disciple of Christ must have the salt of God's royal recipe sweeping through his or her life in order to diffuse it among others. The ingredients for adequate spiritual development are found in the New Testament.

Peter, a disciple and listener on the mountain, grew in spiritual dimension to the point that he later gave this recipe to us to be shared with others as we taste and assimilate the salt ourselves. Peter suggests faith, virtue, knowledge, temperance, patience, godliness, and brotherly kindness (2 Peter 1:5-7).

The teachings of Jesus Christ are as salt. They penetrate clear to the heart. Salt is the grace of God, the power and love of God, the righteousness of Christ, which comes directly from God and flows to others through Christian love. This love is aggressive and diffusive. Love is the principle of action, and when the heart is full of love, it spills out onto others, making life more palatable just as salt flavors good food.

Along with its tastiness, salt is a vital mineral for our bodies. Salt has been used as a healer of physical wounds. The "salt" Jesus is talking about can heal spiritual wounds. Just how does the grain of salt have the saving quality? Well, you see, the power in the "salt" is the Holy Spirit, grace, and love of God at work in a person. The savor is the vital power of Christ's righteousness pervading the life of the Christian.

Madeline muddled amuck in her early years. She was told to "be good," but confusion through an overload of critical instructions left her feeling contrary. Home, school, and church seemed to dictate a squeezed-in style of living that her jolly passion for life could not permit. Red hair cascading down her strong back, deep blue eyes, and a complexion smooth as cream combined to make a beauty that was beheld by many a mischievous masculine eye.

She danced her way through life with not a care in her mind. And yet, a nagging persisted in the back of her mind. Something she could never put her hurried finger on. Never allowing time to be taken for much thought, she developed a good case of chronic loneliness.

Lovely to look upon, as carefree as a kitten, Madeline became game for the field of fellows fighting for her favors. By and by, one fellow won her heart, she fell in love, married, and thought her troubles were over. But as marriage, children, PTA, and the challenge of her job gave her new worries, she busied her body and mind with too much work, burdening herself and her family beyond the point of the outer reaches of normal behavior. And she broke down.

Counselors, doctors, and clergymen were caught up in her calamity. But it was a salty old friend who sustained Madeline on her long, lonely walk uphill as she rebuilt life, returned to her family, and recovered her happy heritage of early years.

What did the salty old friend do that a wonderful husband and even professionals could not do for Madeline? This salty friend was a child of God who had walked with God through overwhelming storms herself. She knew how to come out well and full of seasoning. It is this kind of saltiness Jesus spoke of on the mountain.

God's people on earth are commissioned by the Savior to sprinkle themselves on others. The saving quality of this salt secures salvation for many people, such as Madeline, muddling through life.

Too often the saints themselves, through a sort of half-surrender to God, lose their saltiness and become insipid. Jesus asked, "If the salt have lost his savor [or flavor], wherewith shall it be seasoned?" (Luke 14:34). True love has penetrating qualities. As a child of God opens up to the love of God, the love spills out onto those near him or her. Love magnifies as it is given. The tragedy of a partly-salty person is that he or she muddies up the salt.

Some "saints" misread Jesus' command about salt by reading sugar. A personal experience with sugar diluted my own "saltiness." Some people take off the top of the salt shaker and pour salt down the throat of their children and neighbors, causing a great distaste for religion. It is possible to repel Christianity by pushing "doctrine." Fanaticism clogs the holes in the shaker.

As a man without reasoning, so is a Christian without seasoning. There simply is no remedy for unsavory salt. It shall be cast out. It shall be trodden under foot.

A humble attitude sprinkled with the vital energy of Christ is salt at its best. Unless the salt of the Holy Spirit is in our lives, our "savor" is lost. Our witness becomes worthless.

Sometimes love, power, and the righteousness of Christ are lost from the life of a professed Christian. The only way this person may be "salted" or restored is to return to the Source of life—Jesus Christ.

The conflict of every human heart is painful at best. Any time you have healed another's hurt, your life is certainly more joyous. And loneliness is softened.

Jesus is the Water of Life. By our saltiness, others become thirsty for Jesus—the Living Water.

A Christian has incredible influence on others. When Jesus shakes His salt shaker and we tumble out, be assured He knows where He is shaking us.

A Christian in the home is a Christian everywhere. Careless and hardened people seem difficult to contact, but angels will bless our outreach. Fear of contact dissolves as we work with anyone, anywhere, anytime.

No soul is lightly esteemed by God. The poorest beggar, the richest person, the most famous, the prisoner, the leaders of a nation—all are souls God loves. And He wishes for us to reach out to them. We are His salt.

God often places us with people we would not choose to mingle with. As we follow His guidance, surrendering to His will, we, like Martha at the party, finally realize what a wonderful life we are living.

"Ye are the salt of the earth" (Matt. 5:13).

My God, My God, Why?

"The kingdom of this world is become the Kingdom of our Lord, and of His Christ; and He shall reign for ever and ever ... King of Kings, and Lord of Lords." These sentences are taken from the middle part of the "Hallelujah Chorus" in Handel's *Messiah*.

The glory of the "Hallelujah Chorus" comes as a burst of triumph at the end of part two of the *Messiah* oratorio. This is a musical composition about the birth of Jesus (part one), the suffering and death of Jesus (part two), and the resurrection and future hope for us all (part three).

However, before the rejoicing of the "Hallelujah Chorus" came the suffering. Jesus, the "Lamb of God," came to die for our sins. Jesus could have died in bed anytime in His life, but He chose to be lifted up for all men to see Him. He endured the most hideous death possible. To be nailed on a cross was pain beyond any other pain.

"And I, if I be lifted up from the earth, will draw all men unto me" (John 12:32).

As He was nailed to that cross, the rejection from the very people He came to die for was without equal. The nation He loved so much despised Him and cruelly killed Him.

With a leaded whip, they had torn up His back. Blood streamed from the deep cuts as a result of the whipping. The arrest and mock trial before the chief priests, Pilate, and Herod was a farce. Placing a crown of thorns on His head, mocking Him, and spitting in His face was only the beginning of the torture of that frightful Friday.

The fury and jealousy of the Jewish leaders stirred up the mob of common people with a frenzy that pushed Pilate and Herod to give the nod to His crucifixion.

The story of Jesus' trip from the trial to the cross is well known by most of us. The ending chapters of all four Gospels tell the story (Matt. 26 and 27; Mark 14 and 15; Luke 22 and 23; and John 18 and 19).

The trial, the long walk up the hill to Calvary, and at last the jarring pain of the nails in His hands and feet were only the beginning of Jesus' agony.

"He was wounded for our transgressions ... and with His stripes we are healed. All we like sheep have gone astray ... and the Lord hath laid on him the iniquity of us all" (Isa. 53:5, 6).

The crowd taunted Him, jeered at Him, and scorned Him. They even challenged Him to come down from the cross. Amidst the shouting and mocking, Jesus forgave those who were doing Him wrong: "Father, forgive them; for they know not what they do" (Luke 23:34).

At high noon an intense darkness covered the land. For the next three hours, it was dark and silent. The sun refused to look upon the shameful scene. An extraordinary darkness identified His death, just as an extraordinary light announced His birth. After nearly three more hours, Jesus broke the silence by shouting, "My God, my God, why hast thou forsaken me?" (Matt. 27:46).

The fact was that because Christ took on the sin of the world, God had to abandon His Son or His presence would have spoiled the original plan of salvation. This was equally difficult for His Father. "Behold, and see if there be any sorrow like unto my sorrow" (Lam. 1:12).

At His baptism the Father spoke saying, "This is my beloved Son, in whom I am well pleased" (Matt. 3:17). Throughout His ministry, there were other times where the Son of God heard the Father audibly speak to Him and give Him the assurance of His presence. But now, when Jesus was physically weakened beyond words, no assuring voice from God could be heard. Jesus was totally alone, abandoned by God—His Father.

At the depth of human loneliness, no desertion can match what Jesus experienced as He hung alone on the cross, dying for my sin, for your sin.

Jesus kept hold of God as His God: "My God, my God." Although it appeared that God had forsaken Him, Jesus still clung to the fact that God the Father was *His* God.

There can be no greater love than this.

That Friday afternoon, as Joseph and Nicodemus laid Him in the grave, I'm certain Satan clapped his hands in victory. But the story doesn't end here. The real victory beamed forth as Jesus was resurrected to life on Sunday.

Hallelujah indeed!

Could Ye Not Watch?

Prayer is talking to God. But what do we say to God?

One of my friends who didn't know God prayed, and God answered him the very next day. He prayed, "God, if there is a God out there, show me a better life."

The night before he had been in a fight at the local bar and couldn't really remember it, except for the cuts and bruises and the mysterious broken bar stool in his living room. He was ready to quit the "old life" and was willing to start the journey to get to know God.

If you want to know what to pray, ask God for help getting to know Him—that's what to pray for. Pray for His presence in your life. God wants to be our Friend. God is always on our side. God is always *at* our side, too.

About 2,000 years ago, Jesus Christ was in need of prayer. And He needed prayer partners. Just before His arrest, trial, and death on the cross, Jesus prayed in the Garden of Gethsemane. His prayer was with deepest agony; His human self did not want to die. Who does?

Earlier that night His disciples had been quarreling over who would be the greatest in Jesus' kingdom. As they traveled toward Gethsemane through the grape vineyard, Jesus pointed out that He was the vine and they were the branches (John 15:5). This picture of "connection" is for all of us.

As they arrived at the place of prayer, Jesus took three disciples, Peter, James, and John, to be closer to His prayer spot. He asked the men to pray. Simple request. He told them to watch, be alert, and pray.

Then Jesus went to His special prayer spot. With great drops of blood, He agonized with His Father about His approaching death. He well knew the plan laid out before Him. His human self recoiled at the thought of the cross. Yet, He had been with His Father at the conception of the plan of salvation long before They created planet earth.

He now pleaded, "Father, if it be possible, let this cup pass from me" (Matt. 26:39). That cup was the torturous death, the separation from His Father, the cruel and painful treatment coming up. He needed prayer partners.

Although He prayed to be released from death, He also submitted His will to God and ended His prayer with these words: "Nevertheless not as I will, but as thou wilt" (*Ibid.*). A perfect prayer.

He arose and went to the disciples, and finding them asleep, asked,"What, could ye not watch with me one hour? Watch and pray, that ye enter not into temptation" (Matt. 26:40).

In this hour of the Savior's supreme anguish, Jesus' longed for human companionship. He wanted sympathy and understanding of kindred spirits. Returning to His prayer spot, He again asked the same request of His Father: release from the awful death ahead of Him. But once again He ended His prayer, "Nevertheless Thy will be done."

From personal experience, when I pray the "nevertheless" prayer, God surpasses my wishes or the desires presented in my own puny prayers. We have an awesome Father in heaven who listens to us and deeply cares about us.

When Jesus returned a second time to the disciples, He found them truly anesthetized, paralyzed in a stupor of the soundest sleep. They were experiencing the "curse of spiritual slumber." They slept through their prayer time. They didn't know they needed prayer.

He addressed the self-sufficient Peter: "Simon, sleepest thou? couldst not thou watch one hour? Watch ye and pray, lest ye enter into temptation" (Mark 14:37, 38).

Peter, the disciple who earlier that evening had boasted, "I'll go to prison, even death for You," couldn't even stay awake for one hour. Peter, "the mouth," always talking, now had to listen.

Jesus in His tenderness of great love for Peter and all His disciples said, "The spirit truly is ready, the flesh is weak" (Mark 14:38). That prayer reaches down the centuries to us, too. The "spirit," meaning the higher powers of the mind, and the "flesh," meaning cravings, obsessions, and compulsions, are often at war within each one of us.

Once more, Jesus prays the same prayer. Yet, returning this time, Jesus speaks to them, "Sleep on now ... the hour is at hand ... Rise, let us be going" (Matt. 26:45, 46).

Jesus had been praying and sweating great drops of blood. He was at the bottom of agony, depression, and discouragement. What was His agony? He had no fear of His Father. His agony, stress, and pressure was in regards to meeting the powers of darkness and facing Satan and all his evil ways.

The Father answered Jesus' prayer this way. He said "no" about the cup, but He sent an angel to give Jesus strength to bear the burden on the cross.

We know Jesus gained the victory over the devil on that cross the very next day. And Jesus' victory over sin and death is ours just for the asking, believing, and receiving.

Jesus' "nevertheless" prayer resulted in victory over the devil. And in our prayers when God says, "No," you can be certain He will give His strength to bear whatever burden comes our way. God is always there for us.

And now, the awful moment had come. That moment was to decide the destiny of the world. Such incredible love the Father and His Son had for us!

Jesus arose from His knees victorious, calm, serene, and confident. While Jesus' eleven disciples—His very best friends—slept, Judas had betrayed Jesus. He and all of Jesus' enemies were wide awake as they put their plan into action.

Suddenly light from torches carried by an angry mob rushed in upon Jesus and His disciples in the garden. Judas had given himself up to Satan, and he had no prayer power to resist him. Judas led the mob to Jesus. The mob, made up of the chief priests and elders, approached Jesus as if they were chasing a wild animal.

Jesus was in complete command of the situation. He took His stand. He asked, "Whom seek ye? They answered him, Jesus of Nazareth. Jesus saith unto them, I am he" (John 18:4, 5). No fear, only a complete trust in His Father's strength, was demonstrated to those around Him. His prayer saw Him through.

Prayer could have seen the disciples through, too. But they fell asleep. Fortunately, Christ loved them anyway. And He loves us. We all live in our own self-made prison. Some are behind bars; others are in the open. Regardless of where you are at, Jesus is with you. Prayer teaches us to want God's will for us. Nevertheless.

Teach Us to Pray

I have met so many people who say, "Why pray? My prayers just go to the ceiling and bounce off." I can't imagine that experience because for most of my lifeI have felt that God answers my prayers. Since I was 4 years old, I've gone to church. Even in the kindergarten class where we sang "Jesus Loves Me," somehow I trusted God.

By the time I was in second grade, I realized that God answers our prayers. For me, He seems to have three different answers to my requests. It seems when it must be immediate, He says, "Yes." When the prayer will not give a good result in the end, He says "No, but I have a better way." Then He sometimes says, "Wait."

One prayer I prayed for 17 years was answered to the affirmative, but the wait seemed like it was forever. Once God said, "Now is the time," the joy, laughter, and sparkle in my life was worth the wait.

One time I saw a lady look to the ceiling and say, "We could use a little help here." It was not a "ceiling only" prayer. God answered her prayer beautifully after a bit of difficult experiences first. The joy on her face to the answer of that simple prayer was infectious.

A young mother was having a marvelous experience with her two children. Things were going great. She also looked up to the ceiling and said, "Make this last." Of course, there were some trying times in her life, but God blessed her with the life she asked for.

While driving a long, straight road in New Mexico a few years back, I woke up on the left side of the road going 70 miles per hour. The hypnotic stretch had lulled me to sleep. When my tires hit the noisy bumps on the road, I jerked awake and prayed one word. In fact, I screamed my prayer.

I prayed from my gut: "Help!" That's all I prayed. Soon I was on the right side of the road, shaking, but unharmed. As I assessed my situation, I realized there had been no cars on the road either way. And the bumps on the side of the road had woken me up. My desperate prayer had been answered. I could have swerved, even turned the car over, but that didn't happen, and I was safe.

As I was thinking about writing this, I asked myself, "Joy, what right do you have writing about a subject that many people have written books on?" Prayer is our personal connection with God, which I certainly have, so that's why I am sharing my experience with you.

The main idea that I want to convey is to have the courage to pray, pray, and keep praying until you get your answers. Stay connected with God in pursuit of the answers you need. The following are a lot of ideas about prayer that I have gleaned through the years. Some from personal experiences and books, others from friends, sermons, and even little children.

One thing I have learned is that I like to pray throughout my day. After my specific prayer time in the morning, I talk to God all day long, seeking His presence during my busy day. I am a piano teacher. If a student is having a hard time learning a section of the music, I quietly pray that he or she will get it. It goes better that way.

Here are several selected gems to carry in your pocket. Read them. Try them. Something will work for you. Give it a try. Give it time. Prayer works.

Without God life makes no sense.
Prayer is talking to God.
God wants to be our Friend.
Ask Him to send you the Holy Spirit.
Pay attention to your prayer.

God is always on our side.
The highest result of prayer is getting to know God.
Prayer discovers more of God.
Prayer is a sense of God's presence.
Talk with Him—that is real prayer.

The secret of failure is to see people rather than God.
The Father is beside every struggling soul.
The human heart longs for sympathy in suffering.
You are never out of God's mind.
"Lo, I am with you always" (Matt. 28:20).

Realize that God is there with you.
Listen to His instruction through the Bible.
Fix your eyes on Jesus Christ.
Intercessory prayer (praying for others) is crucial.
Some requests may be delayed to test our faith.

Seek the Giver, not the gift.
Ask God for a grateful heart.
Prayer does not change God's purpose.
But prayer does release His power.

I hope the following Bible texts and quotes will encourage you as you develop a better prayer experience.

- "Not one sincere prayer is lost. Amid the anthems of the celestial choir, God hears the cries of the weakest human being" (*Christ's Object Lessons*, p. 174).
- "The Lord is nigh unto them that are of a broken heart; and saveth such as be of a contrite spirit" (Ps. 34:18).
- "The poor man cried, and the Lord heard him, and saved him out of all his troubles" (Ps. 34:6).
- "Delight thyself also in the Lord: and he shall give thee the desires of thine heart" (Ps. 37:4).

God will answer our prayers immediately for deliverance and pardon from sin. Love is the binding thread of all life and all God's works. It's the work you can do; you can pray. Just remember, the goal of your prayer life is to gain a closer union with God, not get your way or what you want.

More Prayer Gems

Be still and know that He is God.
Find a quiet spot and allow your body to relax.
Pray for others first—family, country, friends.
Pray according to God's will.
Pause in His presence.

The silence of the soul makes more distinct the voice of God.
People of prayer are people of power.
Jesus is the answer for all people.

Pray with intensity.
Use your Spirit-filled life to bless others.

Ask God to take away the fascination of sin.
Prayer is a sense of God's presence.
God understands the broken language of sighs and groans.
Prayer ought to be a therapy session with God alone.

The Father is beside every struggling soul.
Nothing can prevent the spirit of earnest prayer.
Live in the attitude of gratitude. Give thanks.
Prayer is the greatest of all time savers.
Believe God answers. Trust God to answer.

Prayer is the stepping stone into the presence of God.
Unceasing prayer is the unbroken union of the soul with God.
Joy is the sign that forgiveness has happened.
An act of love is prayer in itself.
Prayer must be lived as well as spoken.

My priorities: Seek God; find Him; love Him; trust Him.
Pray for wisdom.
Pray for the Holy Spirit.
Thank God for blessing you.
Wake up praying; go to sleep praying.
Sincere personal prayer is always answered.

As long as we are still trying to straighten out our own lives--apart from Jesus Christ--we will not make it. It is through the all-powerful name of Jesus Christ alone that we can gain victory over trials and temptations. Jesus, Himself said: "I can of mine own self do nothing ... I seek not mine own will, but the will of the Father" (John 5:30).

"You cannot weary [God]" (*Steps to Christ*, p. 100). If we ask Him, God will give us people in the structures of our lives with whom we can share the delight of being alive in Christ. If there is someone who needs a blessing, include that person in your prayers. Prayer is the one form of communication that can take place in your mind. God knows exactly what you are thinking.

When God is living in you and you have a connection to Him through prayer, others will see that in you. Set an example of how a child of God should live. View the outcome of your prayer with optimism.

We live in a world where lots of things don't work right. That's because of sin. When Christ becomes the vitalizing power in my life, then I can resist temptation. Remember that at any moment you can reach out and connect with God through prayer. When this happens, you are in Him and He is in you, and your life is enriched beyond all measure, and you can withstand the temptations that plague you.

Unfortunately, hurry, worry, fear, and doubt often cripple our prayer life. If you feel as if you are slipping, pray for God's grace, mercy, and strength. Heavenly messengers visit homes where the inhabitants regularly spend time in prayer.

Wouldn't you like to wake up each morning and hear, "Good morning, I am God. I'll be handling your problems today. Just trust Me."

You can trust Him! Try it. Remember, God is only a prayer away.

The Sinner's Friend

Condemned. What a terrible word.

Friend. What a wonderful word.

Everyone makes mistakes. Mistakes may or may not have consequences. But a mistake in good judgment could put you behind bars. And a choice of personal conduct may keep you from heaven. If heaven is our goal, we need to know more about our Savior. Will He say "condemned," or will He say "friend," when He returns to this earth?

Paul wrote the following in Romans 7:18: "How to perform that which is good I find not." Here was a very holy man of God, but the apostle Paul struggled with sin just as we all do.

But just a few verses later, he wrote in a relieved tone, "I thank God through Jesus Christ our Lord" (verse 25). He had assurance of God's grace and love through Jesus.

Then in Romans 8:1, he wrote, "There is therefore now no condemnation to them which are in Christ Jesus." When we accept Christ's gift of salvation, we are no longer guilty of sin. Jesus' blood covers us and pays for our mistakes. Later in that same chapter, we find one of my favorite texts: "And we know that all things work together for good to them that love God" (verse 28).

Earlier, in the Gospel of John, we come to a story about a terrified woman who was thrown at Jesus' feet. She had sinned, and the rulers of Jerusalem intended to make an example of her. Also, they delighted in trapping Jesus in a moral trap. As she stood trembling before Jesus, the scribes and Pharisees accused: "Master, this woman was taken in adultery, in the very act" (John 8:4).

It was a very intense moment. This woman was caught. She *was* a sinner. The rulers reminded Jesus, "Now Moses in the law commanded us, that such should be stoned: but what sayest thou?" (verse 5).

These rulers had two goals. One was to create a public display of this sinner. The other was to trick Jesus. If He forgave her outright, Jesus could have been in trouble with the law. on the other hand, if He did not forgive her, then the sentence would stand, which would put Him in trouble with the Roman authorities.

Jesus always had a better way to solve a problem. And this is what He did. They expected action on His part. But Jesus acted as if He did not hear.

However, Jesus was not ignoring them. He was the Son of God and could read their hearts. As He looked at the group of men pointing their fingers at this trembling woman, Jesus read their minds.

Ignoring their scorn, He stooped to write in the sand. Then He stood up and stated, "He that is without sin among you, let him first cast a stone at her" (verse 7). As He wrote each man's sins in the sand, the men slowly disappeared. Jesus, who was the only one without sin, finally stood alone with the woman.

I have always thought Jesus was doubly kind to all the sinners present. The men were yelling and pointing to the woman. Jesus, on the other hand, quietly wrote their sins in the sand. The wind would blow that sand away. He did not publicize the men's sinful hearts. But as they read their own sins, their consciences were stricken. Yes, Jesus dealt with their sins, but they were not publicly embarrassed, as they did with the woman.

I say Jesus was doubly kind because the woman who was left to face her Savior knew she had sinned. She fully expected the stones to snuff out her life. However, Jesus stood up and asked, "Woman, where are those thine accusers? hath no man condemned thee? She said, No man, Lord. And Jesus said unto her, Neither do I condemn thee: go, and sin no more" (verses 10, 11).

What a Friend for that woman. What a Friend we each have. No, He doesn't overlook our sins. He forgives us of our sins. What a Friend, indeed.

Reward

One beautiful spring morning I took a ride in the country. As I drove over a hill, the panorama of a nearby lake took my breath away. I decided to stop for a snack under a shady tree, enjoy the lake, and read a little.

As I settled myself on the ground, my Bible opened to Genesis 15:1. I don't usually take promises God spoke to others as my own, but this popped out at me like a neon sign. "Fear not, Abram: I am thy shield, and thy exceeding great reward."

All my life I had been told that heaven is my "reward." I had my own ideas in my mind of what heaven must be like. Each time I thought about heaven it became more beautiful and more real to me. Yes, I was going to heaven someday.

But as I read this verse, I realized that heaven is not "my goal" after all. It is only the place where God lives. God is my reward and goal in life. "I am … thy exceeding great reward," the Lord told Abraham.

Pondering this text, I came to a conclusion. If God is my reward, and heaven is God's home, and He is inviting me to follow Him now, someday soon I'll live with Him in His home. But He must be my God here and now. Somehow He must be by my side all the time.

Knowing that we each have a personal angel and Jesus promised His Spirit as a gift, the presence of God must be a constant. No matter my life situation, or my geography, no matter where I am or what I'm doing, God is there. That is an awesome thought!

This Generational Thing

One day I was angry at God, and I told Him so. I am a very compulsive person, and I have had a battle with this "sin" all my life. Actually, I suppose all of us have had to battle sin.

This particular morning I was in the right position to talk to God. I was kneeling by my bed. My Bible was open before me. I had been struggling over this particular sin for too long, and I chose to blame one of my grandfathers for my weakness—my bent to this sin.

I complained to the Lord, "Why did You give me R. L. S. as my grandfather?" I was crying. It was a heavy moment in my life. I knew the second commandment said, "For I the Lord thy God am a jealous God, visiting the iniquity of the fathers upon the children unto the third and fourth generation of them that hate me" (Ex. 20:5).

I was feeling the "generational curse," and it was heavy. Opening my eyes, I looked at the tears in my hands and wept some more. Then my gaze went beyond my hands to my Bible.

Here's what I saw: Luke 3:38. "Which was the son of Enos, which was the son of Seth, which was the son of Adam, which was the son of God." This was the last verse on the genealogy of Joseph, Jesus' earthly father.

I read the text again and smiled. Overjoyed at a new thought, I exclaimed, "Well, we all have a genealogy that goes back to Adam, which was the son of God. The son of God. Of God ..."

"Lord," I prayed, "I'm a child of God as much as Adam. R. L. S. just got in the way." I had never seen the past so clearly. R. L. S. was only my human grandfather. God was (and is) my Father, my Maker, and my Creator, and in Him I will live!

Later I returned to Exodus 20:5 and kept reading on to verse 6, which says, "And shewing mercy unto thousands of them that love me, and keep my commandments." Now I was laughing. Both texts fit me. I praise God for this experience. God is my Father. And God is your Father, too.

He Bought Me

I like words that sound alike. Like a poem, they catch my imagination. The other day I was fooling around with words and came up with some rhyming words that pretty-well describe my own life.

He *bought* me—He *sought* me—He *taught* me—He *caught* me—He *fought* for me—He *got* me.

On the cross one cruel Friday long ago, Jesus bought me. He paid the price. He paid the ransom for me. I am bought with a huge price. That price was our Savior's death on the cross. I've been purchased. The price was incredible, almost unbelievable.

The cross is a true fact of history. It was the ultimate act of grace. Hollywood cannot portray the passion scene as well as the Gospels of Matthew, Mark, Luke, and John. The last three chapters of each gospel tell it as it happened.

Jesus paid for everyone's sins when He died on the cross. All have sinned. All have been purchased. Jesus chose each of us, but accepting Jesus' death is our choice.

He Sought Me

Waaa! Waaa! At last I was free to express myself. I wanted to be born at 4 a.m., but the doctor ordered the nurse to stop my mom's labor. At a more convenient time, 11 a.m., the doctor used forceps to bring me into the world. I have had a painful neck all my life as a reminder of that fiasco.

Now, as I look over a very long life, I can see plainly that God was there at my birth. The older I get the more I realize God is always there. Not just for me, but for all of us.

Growing up as an only child for five and a half years, I could have become terribly spoiled. But I thank God that another baby joined our family. My baby brother saved me from becoming the most spoiled person on earth. The center of the universe did not revolve around me anymore.

Even as a young child, God *sought* me to be His own. Before I knew what sin was, I'm certain I plunged into sin just like all children do.

Seeking me, indeed seeking all of us, God must be very busy. But it seems to be the very thing He delights in most. Jesus told us three stories of lost things that were found as examples of how much He seeks after us in an effort to rescue us from sin—a simple coin, one sheep out of 100, and a son of an unnamed rich man (Luke 15).

The first story is about a lost sheep—just one in a flock of 100. In the parable the shepherd leaves the flock that is safe and goes searching, seeking, looking for the one lost sheep. Note that the sheep didn't go searching for the shepherd. The sheep was lost and didn't know what to do about it. Finally, the shepherd found the sheep. Once he did, he placed the sheep upon his shoulders and carried it home, rejoicing that all his sheep were safe.

The next story portrays a home where a woman is searching for one lost coin, out of ten. She told her neighbors about her loss. The coin was lost but obviously didn't know it. She swept the place until she found her lost coin. Then she rejoiced with her neighbors over the one coin found. Jesus is comparing this with the joy that the angels have over one sinner that repents.

The third story is about a son who asked for his inheritance early so he could go off and "have a good time." He spent his father's money, but a drought plagued the land, and he was alone. With no money and no friends, he was hungry and desperate. He longed to be at home once again. The boy was lost and knew it. He also knew what to do about it. He realized his father's servants lived better than he did. He finally returned home.

The father, who had let his son go at his request, allowing him freedom to live how he wanted, watched the dusty road day after day. One day, as the father looked down the road once again, he saw his son approaching. The father had been watching, always searching for him. The boy came home dirty, ragged, and smelly, not at all looking as a rich man's son should look. But the open arms, the best robe, the fatted calf, and the homecoming party all spoke of the love the father had for his prodigal son.

All these stories, each in their own way, describe how God seeks after us. He is there. No matter where on earth we are. God knows exactly where you are and why. He is reaching out His generous and loving arms for you. You are being *sought* after; don't run away.

He Taught Me

In a little church school, Mrs. B., my second grade teacher, was teaching about the plan of salvation. She explained the big words so well that, as a little girl, I understood every word.

Mrs. B. explained that while planning this world in heaven God and His Son discussed the possibility of sin entering in. As they talked about their new creation with great joy, they also discussed the sin-factor, should it arise.

It was there that Jesus volunteered His life for our salvation. Sure enough, after the world was created, Adam and Eve sinned. Eating the forbidden fruit in the Garden of Eden was an expression of their disobedience and disloyalty to God. It was right there in the garden that the Lord laid out the plan for redemption (Gen. 3:15).

The four Gospels tell of the plan of action. Each book ends with Jesus' death on the cross and His resurrection, the fulfillment of the plan and the assurance of eternal life.

Here are the "big words" Mrs. B. explained to us that day:

Salvation: "Thou shalt call His name Jesus: for he shall save his people from their sins" (Matt. 1:21).

Redemption: An act of Jesus on the cross redeeming His people from their sins.

Justification: An act of Jesus on the cross enabling us to stand before God "just as if" we had not sinned.

Sanctification: The work of a lifetime. This represents the choices we make every day.

Righteousness: Doing right.

End of Time: The days just before Jesus returns to earth.

First Resurrection: Redeemed are raised from the dead for their reward—heaven.

Second Resurrection: Sinners are raised from the dead for their reward—hellfire.

Christ's Second Return: Jesus is coming soon to take His faithful people to His home in heaven forever and ever.

At last, Mrs. B. told us about translation. I remember sitting up and listening to that idea. She said, "Some of you in this room will probably be alive when Jesus returns to take you to heaven. You won't see death." Somehow, I got the picture that I might, after all, never die. I liked that thought. We who are alive now may possibly not die if Jesus returns soon. Wow! What a thought! Are you ready?

He Caught Me

When I was 10 years old, we had a pastor who got into my little head. He portrayed a loving God to me. He would stand up and tell the children a story. But he never seemed to finish the story, and since Mom chose to sit in the second row, I listened to the entire sermon.

He wove his sermons around the love of God. Oh, yes, he talked about doctrine, and his sermons were Bible-centered, but somehow as he preached week after week, I came to know that God loved me, just a little girl, and Jesus died for me, as well as everyone else.

About that time my mom felt that I was giggling too much with my friends at church and wasn't acting properly before church. So my mom prayed that I would be a good girl. Shortly after that, we got a call from the kindergarten leader. She needed a pianist, and she asked, "Would Joy play the piano for the kindergarten class?" Mom said, "Yes, of course." After she hung up the phone, she told me about my new responsibility.

Well, I obtained a kindergarten song book and started practicing. Playing that first time was scary for me. But somehow I got through it. After that I practiced very hard for each week's new songs. By and by, I got very good.

Then, one day a teacher of one of the classes didn't show up. The leader asked me to teach the class. Well, I was only 11 years old, but she convinced me that the sand box, felts, coloring books, and crayons were all ready. She handed me the lesson page to read to the kids and left everything in my hands.

I was asked to substitute one other time, and I wasn't so scared the second time. Soon after that the class of six wiggly kindergarten kids became "my kids," and I became their teacher.

As I got more involved in church, I knew I wanted to be baptized. It was time. My pastor came to my home, asked me a lot of questions, and planned my baptism date.

I have always thought that God *caught* me during my younger years, and I have never left God. I don't mean I have never sinned; no, indeed. But each time I get my foot off the straight-and-narrow path, it seems God catches me.

I belong in God's great fishing net. I'm a "keeper" as fishermen say. The longer I live the more grateful I am that I had the right pastor tell it like it is. He gave me God. I was and am very fortunate. Yes, I am blessed.

Peter, one of Jesus' disciples, was a fisherman. Jesus told him and the other disciples, "You have been fishing for fish, but I want you to 'follow me, and I will make you fishers of men'" (Matt. 4:19).

Catch people for the Lord. That's just what my pastor did for me, and I'm one thankful gal. This I know and have known since I was 12 years of age: God loves me; Jesus died for me; and the Holy Spirit works with me and keeps me company. You can experience the same thing. Let God catch you.

He Fought for Me

"I meant what I said." These words came to me two weeks after the Lord had told me that something I was doing was wrong.

He first spoke to me while I was peacefully sitting on a rock overlooking the beautiful Albuquerque area. Watching the sunrise with its many colors turning maroon, crimson, pink, orangey-yellow, and brilliant gold bursting into the fullness of the rays of the sun, God spoke to me. He said that what I was doing was wrong. Astonished, I did some thinking about it. Then, after a bit, I dismissed it, wondering what could be wrong with "that thing."

Two weeks later I was playing the piano in a rehearsal with a 55-voice choir of kids for a Vacation Bible School program. The kids could sing loud. In fact, many of them were shouting. And it was in that situation, along with my very loud piano playing, that I heard, "I meant what I said." It was in the same loving tone of voice, but it was more powerful this time. I nearly fell off the piano bench. I'm not sure how I kept playing. But I did.

It seems that after God bought me, sought me, taught me, caught me He still had a lot to do with me to bring me to the point that He could really save me. His voice was soft the first time, yet strong. Firm, not harsh. Gentle, yet I knew it was God's voice to me. His powerful voice the second time was enough. I said, "Okay, Lord." And I changed my ways. It was hard, but I'm glad I did.

What I have learned out of all this is that we all have temptations. The book of Revelation, the last book in the Bible, says that the victorious and the overcomers are the ones who will inherit eternal life. These are the ones going to heaven. So there must be some kind of something to overcome. There must be a victory over something. That something is certainly sin.

It pays to take a good look at the Ten Commandments, the laws of God (Exod. 20). It pays to look at them often to see how our lives line up with God's law. When you fail, ask God to fight for you. He will help release us from the devil.

When God told me, "I meant what I said," I still had a great battle before I was released from that sin. But God fought for me. He stayed by me as I struggled through and beyond. Oh, how I wish that had been the only sin I had to conquer. But, no, I'm human—there are a lot of battles yet to overcome. The wonderful part is that God is willing to fight the devil with me and for me. God *will* fight for you, too. Give Him a chance to prove He is on your side.

He Got Me

After years of eating too much, I finally signed up for Overeaters Anonymous—a twelve-step program for people who struggle with their weight. The twelve steps have helped me see some things I may have never found. I'm very grateful for the program. And I'm very grateful for the victory within the group.

I always wanted God, and I know He always wanted me. In fact, He always wants each of us. After all, He went to a lot of trouble creating us to begin with. Even thinking about the human race was a magnificent thing for God to do. And redeeming us, saving us from our sins was the most awesome experience on earth.

While attending the twelve-step program, I came across an article written by Dr. Harry Tiebout, M.D., on surrender. In essence, he talked about how surrender is a thing we do in our subconscious—I would call it "in my gut"! Submitting is just not enough. He said, by "superficial yielding, tension still continues." Submission or "trying harder" is just not enough. He went on to say that "an act of surrender is an occasion wherein the individual no longer fights life, but accepts it."

Surrender is the special thing I was missing, and I know a lot of people miss this one thing, too. Surrender to the will of God is the most important thing we can do for ourselves. Each of us has something to "give up"—something that stands in the way of having that close connection with our Maker. It is something special to know that the One who created us and redeemed us on the cross is willing to get us to the place of complete surrender to His will and His way of doing things.

Surrender. Give it a try. Then surrender the next day, and the next day. Finally, you will realize the most wonderful life you can have is yours!

You can find the joy of life no matter where you are, no matter the condition of your life—physical ailments, sorrow, loss of loved ones. Joy is possible for us all.

In prison each person has a lot to yield to God, but once you surrender to His will, life turns around. Your better self shines through. I'm fully convinced that the more you let God into your life the more joy shines on your face. Try it, surrender to the will of God. Let the Lord help you.

"Delight thyself also in the Lord; and he shall give thee the desires of thine heart" (Ps. 37:4).

A Book of Encouragement

"The just shall live by faith" (Rom. 1:17). When Martin Luther discovered this text in the Bible, he finally knew God could love him. He had been trying, like many of us do, to earn God's love.

There is a balance between faith and the law of God. We find that "all have sinned, and come short of the glory of God" (Rom. 3:23.) "For the sinful nature is always hostile to God.... That's why those who are still under the control of their sinful nature can never please God" (Rom. 8:7, 8, NLT).

Yet Romans 8:28 gives us the most encouraging verse we could read. "All things work together for good to them that love God." All things includes everything, your past, your future, and your here and now. I somehow picture my angel scooping up the shattered pieces of my past and taking them to God in heaven where He burns the bad parts up on the altar. I picture Jesus on the cross saying, "Father, forgive Joy, for she knows not what she does" (see Luke 23:34).

"Through the law we become conscious of sin" (Rom. 3:20, NIV). Indeed, "I would not have known what coveting [sin] really was if the law had not said, 'Do not covet'" (Rom. 7:7, NIV).

From time to time, we all wish for the wrong things. But Romans 13:14 strongly states, "Don't ... think about how to indulge your evil desires" (NLT). And Romans 14:7 clearly states that none of us live for only ourselves alone. We all are an influence on others even when we don't recognize that fact. More than influencing people, "we belong to the Lord" (Rom. 14:8, NLT).

"God's kindness leads you toward repentance" (Rom. 2:4, NIV). Paul, the author of Romans, struggled with his own sin and weaknesses. This mighty man of God admits, "I have the desire to do what is good, but I cannot carry it out" (Rom. 7:18, NIV).

As he was wrestling with his sinful nature, he cried out, "Who will rescue me from this body of death? Thanks be to God—through Jesus Christ our God!" (Rom. 7:24, 25, NIV).

Now for one of my favorite texts in the entire Bible. After much wrestling with his sinful nature, Paul declares, "Therefore, there is now no condemnation for those who are in Christ Jesus" (Rom. 8:1, NIV).

Later in the same chapter, he says, "If God be for us, who can be against us?" (verse 31, NIV). And then again in verse 38, he declares, nothing "will be able to separate us from the love of God that is in Christ Jesus our Lord" (NIV).

Talk about encouragement!

Romans 11 talks about "in grafted branches." It reminds me of Jesus' last talk with His disciples just before his experience in Gethsemane. They were walking through a vineyard. And He said, "I am the vine; you are the branches" (John 15:5). I picture myself as a small branch connected to the vine, the Savior Himself. At the place of connection from the vine to the branch, grace flows into the inner being of the branch, the person. The "sap" of grace flows invisibly and silently from the Savior to the person.

But Paul doesn't leave us there. He goes on to present these significant spiritual thoughts. Romans 10:9 says, "If you confess with your mouth, 'Jesus is Lord,' and believe in your heart that God raised him [Jesus] from the dead, you will be saved" (NIV).

Eternal salvation is the prize we all long for. And we long for freedom from sin, no matter the size. Some sins, yes, some crimes, are small. Yet, huge sin and enormous crimes are forgivable in God's eye, as is a "small sin."

Romans 15:4 assures us that "through endurance and the encouragement of the Scriptures we might have hope."

How To Get Along With Others

This is sort of a P. S. from the overview of Romans in the last chapter.

Romans 12 popped out at me one day when it seemed that I could not please anyone. When everything is going wrong, I pray and turn to God's Word for encouragement.

I guess it would be wonderful to be perfect, but I have yet to experience that. Instead, I feel my blunders deeply. Oh to be more like Jesus who managed to say the right thing at the right time. Remember how He handled the touchy situation when the Pharisees threw a woman at His feet who had been caught in adultery? (If you don't remember this story from a previous chapter, read John 8.)

Anyways, I like to think of Romans 12 as the proverbs of the New Testament because it tells us how to get along with others. Verse two says, "Be transformed by the renewing of your mind" (NIV). Of all the parts of our body, the mind seems to function first. As a piano teacher, I've watched students sort of daydream, partially tuning out the music and not really making music at all. When I "bring them back" to the music, their mind is once again in control of the fingers, the eyes, and the ears. Their mind is "renewed."

In our spiritual life, there are fixed pathways between brain cells formed over years of undisciplined thinking. In order for our mind to be "renewed," there needs to be new connections between the brain cells. Jesus the Healer can grant us the miracle of a renewed mind. He says, "Ask and you will receive" (John 16:24, NIV).

Romans 12:3 certainly eliminates conceit when it suggests, "Do not think of yourself more highly than you ought" (NIV). Verse 9 tells us that "love must be sincere" (NIV).

I like verse 12 and 13: "Be joyful in hope, patient in affliction, faithful in prayer.... Practice hospitality" (NIV).

Hospitality is one thing we can do all the time. A pleasant encounter, perhaps a courteous "hello," a smile, or a deeper companionship with friends is hospitality on a perpetual basis. Of course, inviting people into your home is not always possible, but inviting them into your heart is a great way to "get along with others."

Here's one that's difficult. "Bless those who persecute you; bless and do not curse" (verse 14, NIV). Whoa! That's hard. But it's worth trying. And you know, it works!

"Rejoice with those who rejoice; mourn with those who mourn" (verse 15, NIV). Jesus did this very thing. His first miracle was at a wedding where He turned the water into wine. And when his friend Lazarus died, Jesus wept. His tears joined Mary's and Martha's.

Verse 16 and 18 say, "Do not be proud ... Do not be conceited.... If it is possible, as far as it depends on you, live at peace with everyone" (NIV).

And Paul's final piece of advice for getting along with others is this: "Do not be overcome by evil, but overcome evil with good" (verse 21, NIV).

Give it a try. It works!

Born on Death Row

The first two chapters in the Bible, Genesis 1 and 2, tell of the beginnings of all things on earth. Words cannot describe the beauty of the Garden of Eden. The animals were tame, even friendly. One could see millions of stars in the clear night sky. There was no pollution or disease.

As a matter of fact, a lot of things were not there in that perfect garden. No closets with the early morning stressful moment to pick out the right clothes in a hurry. Adam and Eve were clothed in a robe of righteousness. No thorns on the roses. No crying, except possibly tears of joy. The leaves stayed green. The flowers did not droop or fade. Sadness was absent from that lovely garden. Death was unheard of. Adam could put his arm around the lion's neck without fear. The wolf romped with the lambs. It was a safe society, indeed.

The last two chapters of the Bible, Revelation 21 and 22, describe a new heaven and a new earth as a new beginning for those who are victorious over evil and have overcome personal sin with God's help. The beauty of it is that God Himself is our "exceeding great reward" (Gen. 15:1).

Eden and heaven—wonderful beyond your imagination; better than any dream we may have. But, and this is an ugly part, the third chapter of Genesis tells the tragic story of how Eve ate the fruit the serpent tempted her with. Soon after, Adam also ate the forbidden fruit. And in a sense, the rest of the Bible deals with sin and its remedy.

Thanks to Adam and Eve and the first sin, we are all born on "death row." When Adam and Eve were sent out of their beautiful garden, they saw the first leaves fall from the trees. Death was now a fact. Tears of sorrow began to flow.

By and by, Cain, their first child, was born. Temporary joy soothed the sorrow. Able, their second son, was a delight for them all of his short life. Then right there in the very beginnings of this world, jealousy and sibling rivalry destroyed the happiness they had when Cain killed Abel.

Abel was dead. Cain had to move away. Genesis 3:15 was the promise that the people of the Old Testament times lived for. Seth, the third child born to Adam and Eve, became the first child of promise. Later on, Isaac, Abraham's promised child, was born. The story of King David and his kingly ancestors is well known. Down through the years, that promise—the promise of a Savior—kept the Jewish nation looking forward. Isaiah and other prophets foretold details about that promised Person.

Finally, Jesus Christ was born in Bethlehem of Mary, a virgin, and the promise was fulfilled. His birth, life, death, and resurrection are detailed in the Gospels of Matthew, Mark, Luke, and John. Each book reveals Jesus Christ.

When the final moments of our Savior arrived, He was nailed between two thieves. One of them was sorry for his life of sin. He recognized he had been born on death row, and he wanted to escape. As he turned to Jesus, he knew Jesus was no criminal. No, He was the Son of God. By asking Jesus for a place in His eternal kingdom, this thief knew for certain that he would ultimately be in heaven. Heaven was his request, and his request was granted.

The other thief was still on death row. He died without hope, and he will someday be resurrected to simply be destroyed in the great lake of fire.

We each have a choice. Stay on death row or give our hearts to the Lord. With gratitude, sorrow for our sin, and a new commitment to God, our repentance will take us from death row and ultimately give us that wonderful opportunity to live a life free from sin and death.

Keep Getting Up

As human beings we seem to be addicted to the sin of our choice. Yet, we desire heaven for our eternal home. There's a big gap there. What to do? What to do?

James 1:2-4 in the *Amplified Bible* translates the verses in this way: "Consider it wholly joyful, my brethren, whenever you are enveloped in or encounter trials of any sort or fall into various temptations. Be assured and understand that the trial and proving of your faith bring out endurance and steadfastness and patience. But let endurance and steadfastness and patience have full play and do a thorough work, so that you maybe [people] perfectly and fully developed [with no defects], lacking in nothing."

Trials can knock us down, but no one can live without trials. Likewise, we cannot live without temptations. Temptations come in many forms and are themselves *not* the sin. The devil knows just how to entice us with the "sin of our choice." James encourages us to consider these temptations joyful.

I often think that the strength we gain through hardships and resisting sinful choices is cause for rejoicing. I remember when life was tough for me in my younger years. It was during one of those tough times that I read about King David and the trials he went through in his earlier life before he was crowned king. He was fleeing from King Saul. He and his men were being relentlessly pursued, living in caves to survive, running, running, always running. With some of my earlier trials, I felt I was also running from situations too great to deal with.

One morning I read 2 Samuel 22:30. "For by thee I have run through a troop: by my God I have leaped over a wall." This is pretty descriptive. There seems to be a way of escape as we recognize that God can help us leap over the wall of our trials or temptations. Verse 37 describes further help from the Lord. "Thou hast enlarged my steps under me; so that my feet did not slip." Yet, our sinful choices get us into big trouble, and we often slip.

Here again, the Scriptures assure us: "The steps of a good man are ordered by the Lord: and he delighteth in his way. Though he fall, he shall not be utterly cast down: for the Lord upholdeth him with his hand" (Ps. 37:23, 24).

God knows us very well—each of us. After all, we are His creation, His creatures.

He knows that we will fall as children of Adam and Eve. That's why our Savior came to earth to die for our sins.

Sin is slippery. It's sneaky. It slips up on us. It seems the secret lies in what we do when we fall into temptation. I often picture myself running, slipping, and facing God as I get up and run into the arms of God. As long as I'm facing toward God, the race is a race of true victory. However, when I'm so foolish as to run away from God, then I know I'm in trouble.

Proverbs 24:16 perfectly describes the solution. "For a just man falleth seven times, and riseth up again: but the wicked shall fall into mischief."

Micah 7:8 even expresses joy in the process of falling and rising again. "Rejoice not against me, O mine enemy: when I fall, I shall arise."

Keep getting up.

Freedom From the Flames

A cold chill shook Marcia as the speaker described the flames of hell. She was sure that she deserved hell as punishment for the life of crime she was living. The evil she was involved in was her choice—it was her way of life. Yet, there lingered in her heart a yearning to be free from her life of crime.

Martin, her best friend, caught up with her as she walked home after listening to this very descriptive lecture on hell. His eyes were sparkling. She had never seen him look happy before. And in her misery she couldn't understand this glow of happiness.

"Isn't it awesome, Marcia?" beamed Martin.

"What's so awesome?" Marcia snapped back.

"Well, when the speaker said, 'There is a way out of hell,' I just couldn't believe it. You and I have been hell-bent for most of our lives. But when this speaker said, 'There is a way to be free from the flames,' I just knew there is a chance for you and me to change our lives, to be forgiven and on God's side at last. We can have freedom from the flames."

"All I heard about," Marcia yelled at Martin, "was how hot hell will be. I really quit listening after that."

But Martin's radiant face caused Marcia to pause. She realized that something significant was going on in Martin's magnificent mind. At least she thought his mind was magnificent. He was always the mastermind behind their many episodes of crime. And she was always an eager participant to their life of evil.

The speaker had talked about this "way of escape." He called it grace. Webster's

Dictionary describes grace as a "virtue coming from God, an unmerited gift from God." We do not deserve grace, but it is God's gift to us if we will only take it. Grace gives us freedom from hell. It means favor to one who is undeserving.

In the book *Steps to Christ*, the author Ellen White presents a clear picture about this freedom from hell: "In the matchless gift of His Son, God has encircled the whole world with an atmosphere of grace as real as the air which circulates around the globe. All who choose to breathe this life-giving atmosphere will live and grow up to the stature of men and women in Christ Jesus" (p. 68).

Happiness is a quality of life we all reach for. Many people are so tormented by their failures and sins that their sense of personal worth is shattered. Many diseases come from a troubled conscience.

One of the encouraging things in the Bible is that it's never too late to start over. The book of Hosea tells of God's expansive love for sinners. This is a book worth reading!

Look at the following verses that demonstrate God's love and plan for us: "For I know the plans I have for you," declares the Lord, "plans to prosper you and not to harm you, plans to give you hope and a future" (Jer. 29:11, NIV). "See, I have engraved you on the palms of my hands" (Isa. 49:16, NIV).

The cross is not in vain for us if we choose our Lord and turn from evil. And the cross is what grace is all about. The cross of Christ lifts us above the future flames of hell and gives real hope for eternal life, a life of beauty forever.

God is the Designer in your life. You cannot buy the grace He offers you. It is a free gift won at the cross. You come to appreciate the grace you have been given most when you get to know the Designer intimately. This personal acquaintance can be gained quickly as you make new choices.

The speaker commented in the presentation Marcia had listened to that "hell is very real. It has terminal effects. Grace is also real. It gives everlasting life. The choice is ours." Freedom from the flames is ours by choice.

Calvary guaranteed our "fire insurance." The insurance policy is signed with the blood on the cross. This gift is ours, no matter our life of past sin. This gift must be accepted by us to be effective in our lives.

With a happy face, Martin pulled Marcia's mind to the Lord as he shared the portions of the sermon that he remembered. He said, "Marcia, the good news is that everything comes out all right."

After all, God decided that people are worth saving, even at the cost of Calvary. With Jesus in your heart, you'll never be lonely again. You are adopted into the family of God. That is pure grace. Embrace it.

God's Will Versus Self-Will

Praying "Thy will be done" but doing just as you please are a dichotomy!

In the Garden of Gethsemane, as Jesus prayed, "Not my will, but thine, be done," He followed through (Luke 22:42). Jesus didn't want to die, but He wanted us to be saved. And the cross of Calvary was the only way. His prayer for escape, "Father, if Thou be willing, remove this cup from me," became "nevertheless not my will, but thine, be done" (*Ibid.*).

In heaven, long before the earth was created, the Father, His Son, and the Spirit of God laid the plans for salvation should Adam and Eve "blow it." Now Jesus was at the final edge of this plan as it was being fulfilled. And indeed, Jesus was crucified the next day after that night spent in prayer.

His "nevertheless" prayer is a pattern for how we should pray. He followed through. He really lived within God's will. We humans often "blow it" just as our first parents did in the Garden of Eden.

God's will versus self-will. Jesus knew God's will. Too many people only guess what God's will is. Can there be a guideline to knowing God's will? Yes, there is. Many Bible texts point the way to God's will. Here are some of them:

"This is the Father's will ... that every one which seeth the Son, and believeth on him, may have everlasting life: and I will raise him up at the last day" (John 6:39, 40).

"Wherefore be ye not unwise, but understanding what the will of the Lord is" (Eph. 5:17; see also verses 19-33).

Paul is writing to the Colossians reminding them how he prayed for them: "For this cause we also ... pray for you, and to desire that ye might be filled with the knowledge of his will in all wisdom and spiritual understanding" (Col. 1:9).

"Now the God of peace ... make you perfect in every good work to do his will, working in you that which is well pleasing in his sight" (Heb. 13:20, 21).

Do "the will of God from the heart" (Eph. 6:6). We see "doing the will of God" as vital to our connection with the Lord. But what is the "will of God"?

"Let us, who are of the day, be sober. putting on the breastplate of faith and love; and for an helmet, the hope of salvation.... Wherefore comfort yourselves ... And be at peace among yourselves. Now we exhort you to be patient toward all men.... Rejoice evermore. Pray without ceasing. In every thing give thanks ... Quench not the Spirit.... Abstain from all appearance of evil" (1 Thess. 5:8-22).

There are so many other Bible verses that address the will of God. Your favorite version will make these verses clear to you.

"For it is God which worketh in you both to will and do of his good pleasure" (Phil. 2:13). Some good advice is to "watch and pray, that ye enter not into temptation: the spirit indeed is willing, but the flesh is weak" (Matt. 26:41).

David longed to do God's will, but he was not a perfect man. Indeed, he murdered Uriah and took Bathsheba, Uriah's wife, as his own. But his desire was to do the will of God. When his self-will overcame him, he prayed for forgiveness and God forgave him. He wrote in Psalm 143:10, "Teach me to do thy will ... lead me into the land of uprightness."

When you have sinned, remember Psalm 51. This is the prayer King David wrote in his book of Psalms after he had sinned. "The prayer of David after his fall, illustrates the nature of true sorrow for sin. His repentance was sincere and deep. There was no effort to palliate [excuse] his guilt; no desire to escape the judgment threatened, inspired his prayer. David saw the enormity of his transgression; he saw the defilement of his soul; he loathed his sin. It was not for pardon only that he prayed, but for purity of heart. He longed for the joy of holiness—to be restored to harmony and communion with God This was the language of his soul: ... 'Have mercy upon me, O God.... Create in me a clean heart, O God.... Cast me not away from Thy presence; And take not Thy Holy Spirit from me. Restore unto me the joy of Thy salvation....'

"A repentance such as this, is beyond the reach of our own power to accomplish; it is obtained only from Christ" (*Steps to Christ*, pp. 24, 25).

When you have sinned deeply, but you really want God in your life, turn to 1 John 1:9: "If we confess our sins, he is faithful and just to forgive us our sins, and to cleanse us from all unrighteousness."

The supreme aim of life is to do God's will. To conclude let's read Proverbs 16:7: "When a man's ways please the Lord, he maketh even his enemies to be at peace with him." And this little gem is found in Micah 6:8: "what doth the Lord require of thee, but to do justly, and to love mercy, and to walk humbly with thy God." I especially like how *The Message* Bible records this same verse: "Do what is fair and just to your neighbor, be compassionate and loyal in your love. And don't take yourself too seriously—take God seriously."

Christian Magic

The crowded bus lurched forward. We all stepped backward. Unfortunately, the heel of my left shoe came down on Suzie's foot. She let out a scream of pain. Instead of going to work that day, the bus took her to the hospital. Yes, indeed, she had broken a bone.

We were new friends, and for ten minutes each morning, we would chat about little things. The friendly banter chipped away the monotonous minutes of our commute.

But the day after the accident, instead of a smile on her face, she lowered her head and glowered at me. If looks could actually kill, I'd be dead.

Day after day, no more smiles, no more chatter, no more "nice girl." Although not my fault or intension, the heal of my left shoe had come down so hard on her foot that something had to give, and it was her bone. I felt terrible. She felt angry. The deed was done. That was that! But it wasn't the end of it.

Bus ride after miserable bus ride came and went. In vain, I tried to get her to smile again or at least to speak to me. But no, she just gave me the early morning angry stare.

Finally, when I could take it no more, I thought of the "magic" of the power of prayer. For ten minutes each morning, as I watched her smolder, I silently prayed for God to forgive her, and me. Then I returned a smile for her scowl. As her foot healed, so did her testy mood. And one day, she returned a smile. That was the beginning of a true friendship.

Someone once said, "When the love of God is enshrined in the heart, like sweet fragrance, it cannot be hidden."

The magic of Christianity comes from Christ when He said, "Love your enemies, bless them that curse you, do good to them that hate you, and pray for them which despitefully use you" (Matt. 5:44). It really works.

The Ultimate Christmas Gift

December is the month that most children look forward to. There are gifts, toys, clothes, and Christmas stockings. There is delight in the eyes of children all over the world.

But Christmas is more than receiving gifts. For those who think about it, the greatest gift is Jesus Christ. The most tragic thing in the world is to *not* accept your greatest gift.

Does this gift come in a box with a red satin ribbon on it? Oh, no, this gift came to us 2,000 years ago in a rude building where beasts were sheltered, in a stable. And the Christ Child was laid in a manger, in a pile of hay—a most humble beginning.

This gift was announced by the angels in heaven. They sang about Jesus' birth. Simple shepherds were talking about and praying for the Promised Savior to come.

Suddenly, they heard the songs about the greatest gift on earth. They followed the angels' instructions to the place of Jesus' birth, and they were the first to bow down in worship to the Holy King, the heavenly gift.

Magi, wise men from the East, followed a special star to where Jesus was. They brought gifts to Jesus, and in return, they received the gift of honoring Jesus.

The gift grew up, and as a young boy, He worked with His earthly dad in the carpenter shop. And when the time was right, Jesus began His public work of teaching, healing, and preaching. He chose twelve men to work with Him. These men later on scattered across the world and shared their experience with the gift, bringing thousands of people to Jesus Christ.

How can a modern-day person accept the gift, and acknowledge the value of this most treasured gift?

Before Jesus finished His earthly work, He did the one thing that can change your life for eternity. He allowed the Roman soldiers to nail Him to a cross. While He died there, hanging on the cross, the mob of people at the foot of the cross jeered, sneered, yelled, and cursed at Him.

At the time of His death, women cried and His mother, Mary, watched as her dear Son was dying. After He said, "It is finished," He dropped His head and died. A Roman soldier gazed up in awe and said, "Truly this was the Son of God" (Matt. 27:54).

His death is our gift. As we, in our minds, look up into His face of agony, to our greatest gift, we see freedom in *our* lives. Freedom from the tyranny of sin. Freedom from the clutches of the devil. We see the possibility of a future life with Jesus, our Savior forever and ever.

He takes us as we are with our blemishes, sins, crimes, mistakes, everything. He loves us. He wants us. And we need Him. Yes, if we choose Him, we will see Jesus in the flesh in our eternal home in heaven.

Many people turn away from the gift. What a tragedy. But you, dear reader, can accept the simple challenge to look to Jesus. This is how you can accept and receive the gift.

Isaiah 45:22 states, "Look unto me [Jesus], and be ye saved, all the ends of the earth." Anyone can look at this gift. If our gift had been buried that Friday, there would have been nothing to "look at." But, no, Satan could not hold the tomb shut. On Friday, Jesus died and was buried. On Sabbath, He rested. Sunday morning, Jesus, our precious gift, was resurrected from death to eternal life. He is the Savior of us all.

God's love for each of us is incredible, awesome. Every human is a sinner. Jesus died for all of us. Eternal life comes only through our faith in Him.

Jesus took our sin and died in our place. "For by grace are ye saved through faith … it is the gift of God" (Eph. 2:8). God only asks for you to simply believe that Jesus died for you and accept Him as your own personal Savior—the greatest gift. Believe and accept. Then believe and accept each new day. Live with godly radiance on your face, joy in your heart, and a message on your tongue. You have a new *gift*—one to share—a gift now and forever.

Stand Still

Good King Jehoshaphat was single-minded in following God. As King of Judah he was loyal to God and highly respected by his people. Also, he was a man of courage. When in trouble, he ran to God first, not through weakness, but to attain God's great strength and direction.

One day he was alarmed to hear that three kingdoms were marching toward Jerusalem in battle to conquer God's Holy Land. The soldiers were from Moab, Ammon, and Mount Seir. The people of Judah came to Jehoshaphat for help, and he proclaimed a fast. Although the Israelites had an army of more than a million strong, he chose to depend on the Lord. The people joined with their king in fasting and prayer.

In Jehoshaphat's very long prayer, he humbly stated, "We don't know what to do. Our eyes are upon You" (see 2 Chron. 20:12). Then the priest, Jahaziel, responded: "Attention … Don't be afraid; don't pay any mind to this vandal horde. This is God's war, not yours. Tomorrow you'll go after them … You won't have to lift a hand in this battle, just stand firm … watch God's saving work for you to take shape. Don't be afraid, don't waver … God is with you" (2 Chron. 20:14-17, *The Message*).

Years earlier, King David had advised, "Be still, and know that I am God" (Ps. 46:10). Now the priest said, "Just stand firm."

Being still before the Lord seems to be the key for His action even in our personal battles. We are to live without fear and trust the Lord.

God's people followed His instructions. The musicians marched first; the army followed the singers. Indeed, it was a unique way to conquer the enemies. "Give thanks to the Lord, His love never quits" was the theme of their song.

When God's people came to the desert of Tekoa where their enemies were, the Lord had set ambushes against these three kingdoms. Behold, their enemies were all dead. They had slaughtered themselves. Not one had escaped.

Imagine the great relief of God's people! No war, complete victory, and no harm to even one of God's people.

Now when the other surrounding kingdoms got word that God had destroyed Israel's enemies for them, the fear of God descended on them. They even brought gifts of silver and huge flocks to Jerusalem.

The Lord gave peace and rest from war to Jehoshaphat and the people of Judah for many years. The spirit of praise renders God's people invincible. Let God fight your battles!

Always on His Case

It seemed the leaders of Israel were on Jesus' case all the time. They plagued Him with questions, trying to stump Him and catch Him slipping up. They hated Him so much, jealous of His success among the common people. They pounded on Him verbally all through His three and a half years of ministry.

In one story, the Publicans collecting the temple tax were at Him. They poked fun of Him, trying to make Him look bad. This time, it was over the question of taxes or tribute money. They challenged Him as to whether He paid tax or not.

But Peter, impulsive Peter, opened up his mouth, and said, "Yes, of course we pay tax."

Jesus' logical response was, "What thinkest thou, Simon? of whom do the kings of the earth take custom or tribute? of their own children, or of strangers?" Simon Peter answered, "Of strangers." Jesus' response was, "Then are the children free" (Matt. 17:25, 26).

However, the rabbis chose to set aside Jesus' claim as prophet and teacher and treat Him as a commonplace person.

Once again, watch the clever way Jesus revealed His glory and "fought this battle." He must have laughed within Himself as He asked Peter to go fishing. He said to Peter, "Go thou to the sea, and cast a hook and take up the fish that first cometh up; and when thou hast opened his mouth, thou shalt find a piece of money: that take, and give it unto them for me and thee" (verse 27).

The leaders of Israel must have been surprised at Jesus' ways and means to obtain the tax money. He was Creator of all fish on the fifth day of creation. Yes, indeed, if He could create a fish, He could place a coin in the mouth of one. Jesus had divine power over nature. He still does.

For a long time in my life, I have read what God and Jesus did to fight the battles of life. As Creator, He could and still can do anything. As we read the Bible about the Lord's many ways of fighting a battle, I have a growing tendency to turn over my battles to the Lord. When I try to do it on my own, I botch it up every time. When I give it to God, what a wonderful life I have, living in the arms of God, seeing His will and His way, in His time, as it unfolds. Some battles are won quickly; some take time.

God bless you as you think about giving God your battles, letting go of them, releasing them, and watching how He fights for us.

All Fall Down

"Joshua fought the battle of Jericho." Or did he?

Yes, Joshua led the children of Israel, but it was God who worked His miracle to conquer the town of Jericho so the chosen people could move on and obtain the Promised Land for themselves.

Israel had been freed from slavery in Egypt through another miracle event at the Red Sea. They had spent forty long years wandering in the desert with the promise in their minds. Traveling toward Canaan, the land God had promised to Abraham and his children, their thoughts were on the land of milk and honey—a land of plenty.

Then they arrived at the river Jordan, and once more, God provided dry land across the rushing water. Now, as they faced the first city they had to conquer, God talked to their leader, Joshua.

Jericho was virtually the key to the whole country. The city was a formidable obstacle to the success of Israel.

All through their desert travel, Moses had been their leader. But he had died, and now Joshua was the chosen leader. The Lord Himself talked to Joshua and laid out a very unusual plan. To his credit, Joshua followed God's instructions, and the people listened to Joshua. They did exactly what God wanted, and it worked.

Listen to the plan: God told Joshua to have the people march in silence around the entire city of Jericho one time each day for six days in a row. On the seventh day they were to walk around, still in silence, but this time they were instructed to walk around seven times.

At the end of the last walk around the city, they were to shout and blow the trumpets of ram's horns, and the walls of this proud, godless city came tumbling down.

The walls were solid and very thick—they were so wide that two chariots could ride on the top side by side. They were well protected inside Jericho, yet, God in His own way shook the ground so no part of the city was left standing.

The men of Israel ran toward the city, which was a heap of rubble. Only one family had been protected. It so happened that there was a prostitute who protected the two spies who, earlier on, had arrived in the town of Jericho. Risking her life,

Rahab had taken them to her home, hid them, and saved their lives.

She had then asked for protection for herself and her family. Rahab made herself available to God, and she became a woman of faith. Pushing past her negative lifestyle, Rahab did not allow her past to rob her of a new beginning.

As the walls came tumbling down, certain Israelite men went to Rahab's place and took her and her entire family to a protected place outside the town. Her life took on a beautiful transformation. King David was one of her descendents, and Matthew 1:5 mentions Rahab as being in the genealogy of Jesus Christ.

Hebrews 11:30 tells us that "by faith the walls of Jericho fell down." God fought that battle! Through faith the children of Israel obeyed the directions of the Lord, and the battle was a success. God will do great things for those who trust His plan.

Remember, let God fight your battles!

Released From Prison

Peter, the bold, mouthy disciple of Jesus, became a great speaker for the Lord after Pentecost. The disciples had spent some quiet time in the upper room talking about all Jesus had done while on earth, and they were all of one mind. Their complete focus was on Jesus Christ. On day forty the Holy Spirit entered the room and entered each of their hearts. This event changed all the disciples, giving them power to preach and heal just as Jesus had while on earth.

Peter became a bold speaker. In fact, 3,000 people were baptized in one day as a result of his sermons. The priests and high priests were not happy with Peter, and after warning him to keep his mouth shut, Herod finally put him in prison and planned to kill him the next day.

Well, Peter, trusting God to take care of him, fell asleep between two guards. While Peter slept, a very devout group of people prayed for him. They prayed for his safety, protection, and very life.

God was fighting this battle, but the praying people did not know the end result. Peter was sound asleep, but God was at work. An angel entered the prison, tapped Peter on the side, and motioned for him to be quiet. He told him to get up, put on his sandals, and come with him. Chains fell from Peter's hands, and they walked through closed gates noiselessly. Then the angel disappeared. Peter, astonished, walked to John Mark's home. He knocked on the door.

A young girl named Rhoda answered the door. She was astonished to see Peter. They were in the very process of praying for his release. Now here he stood at the gate. She did not open the door; instead she left him standing outside, continuing to knock.

Finally, the people responded to Rhoda's story. They went to the door and shouted in surprise and praise upon seeing Peter. He gestured to be quiet. They let him in, had prayer, and Peter left town.

Now, how many people are released from prison in that manner? Just one—Peter.

The book of Acts in the New Testament is full of such stories. God was certainly at work fighting the battles for His people as the early church was established.

You can read this story in its entirety in Acts 12.

Trapped

God's chosen people had been badly mistreated for more than 200 years. And they were crying out to God for help. You see, after Abraham, Isaac, and Jacob lived to ripe old ages, their children and children's children came on the scene. God promised Abraham that his "seed" (also called offspring or descendants) were in line to inherit the land of Canaan.

Abraham's grandson Jacob had twelve boys who were in line to inherit the Promised Land. However, ten of the boys hated Joseph, their younger brother, so much that they threw him in a pit, leaving him there to die. While Joseph was in the pit, a band of Ishmaelites passed nearby, inspiring the brothers to make a little money and sell their brother. For twenty pieces of silver, they sold Joseph. Imagine that!

Well, the God of promises was alert and present with young Joseph. He was sold as a slave to Potiphar, a head honcho in the Egyptian kingdom of the Pharaoh. And Joseph proved himself to be a worthy worker. He was so good at his work that Potiphar put him in charge of all his household.

One day, as fate would have it, Potiphar's wife tried to entice him into her bedroom. Leaving his outer garment as he fled, he exclaimed, "how then can I do this great wickedness, and sin against God?" (Gen. 39:9). But the conniving woman told a bald lie about Joseph and had him imprisoned.

Next we find this fine lad of noble character in charge of the prison and all the prisoners. He was of such a pure character that the keeper of the prison could trust him (see the full story in Gen. 39).

In all, Joseph served for approximately thirteen years in the prison. Then Pharaoh had a dream. Joseph was called to interpret the dream. In this dream Joseph explained that a seven-year period of great plenty would be in the land, followed by seven years of famine. As he explained this dream, Joseph gave God full credit for interpreting the dream.

Because Joseph seemed to be so discreet and wise, he was elected to run the land, saving grain from the seven years of plenty and distributing the extra grain during the seven years of drought.

The famine caused Joseph's brothers to travel down from their home in the land of Canaan to Egypt to receive grain for their families and Jacob, their father. This particular story is so very unusual, and a bit entangled, that I encourage you to read it in Genesis chapters 39 through 45.

In the end, Jacob and his sons, their families, flocks, and children traveled to Egypt to live while the famine continued. There were only seventy members of Jacob's family in all. The Pharaoh gave Joseph's family land in Goshen, a place good for raising sheep (Gen. 46 and 47).

As time went on, Jacob died. Joseph and his brothers grew old and died, too. After Joseph's death, he was no longer remembered in the palace, and the children of God soon had so many children that they were becoming a large nation.

At that time, Pharaoh was building a pyramid and needed slave labor, so he picked this family to become his workers. He didn't know Joseph, nor did he care about Jacob's descendants. The slave drivers beat the children of Israel and severely abused them. The Israelites started crying out, "Help!" God heard.

After more than 200 years of painful slavery in Egypt, God delivered them. He had a plan. After ten dramatic plagues, God's people were finally released to go home.

The next chapter will tell the rest of this story and how God fought their battle for them.

Freed

We will see how God's plan always works best, although it may seem a bit strange while living *in* His plan.

As the children of Israel were crying out for help, God was in the process of delivering the entire race. There were at least 600,000 men, plus their families and their flocks, which made for a huge number of people and animals to be delivered from the Pharaoh and his slave drivers. (Some commentators declare that more than two million came out from Egypt.)

Exodus 1 through 14 tells the exciting story about the ten plagues and ends with the final command from the Pharaoh to get out of his country. And on a very special night that the Jews called the Passover, they all left.

After the Pharaoh and his officers collected their thoughts and realized they had sent their workers out of the land, they changed their minds, quickly got into their chariots, and followed the Israelites into the desert.

Exodus 14:3 says, "For Pharaoh will say of the children of Israel, They are entangled in the land, the wilderness hath shut them in."

Meanwhile, Moses, the leader of the Hebrews, was leading this huge mass of people and animals back to the Promised Land. Walking over the dusty trail must have been hard enough, but when the Red Sea was before them and mountains were on either side and they could go no farther, they panicked.

Fear gripped them as they realized they could not move forward. Then they looked back and saw a huge cloud of dust. The Egyptians had followed them to take them back to Egypt. They were trapped. It seemed like escape was impossible. However, they were about to find out how God works.

Calling upon God to deliver them, Moses asked God what to do. God instructed Moses to strike the Red Sea with his rod. Moses listened to God. If only we would listen to God as easily as Moses did, could it be that God would fight our battles in a spectacular way, also? And can it be that we fail to recognize how God is actually fighting battles for us each day?

Well, as Moses struck the Red Sea with his rod, a most amazing thing happened. The sea piled up on both sides, making a large dry path that was passable for the Hebrews and their flocks.

Just ahead of the Egyptian soldiers, the last of the Hebrews arrived on the safe side of the Red Sea. Now, here's the way God really got involved in this battle. Indeed, He was involved from the beginning as they were crying for help, but can you imagine the terror of the people as they looked back and saw this mass of soldiers racing toward them? At least that was what worried the Israelites.

But plans in God's hands are so spectacular. God instructed Moses to stretch out his rod once again toward the Red Sea. As the soldiers marched and rode their chariots on the dry path the Hebrews had just walked over, the sea suddenly closed up and started to run smoothly in its course. The amazed Hebrews watched as every one of their enemies was drowned in the sea. The chariot wheels were stuck in the sand, and the soldiers and horses were drowned. Every part of the Egyptian plan was foiled. All evil intentions were left behind.

Now, after that dramatic deliverance, Moses and the people sang. Miriam, Moses' sister, led the women in songs. The joy, relief, and astonishment must have been beyond imagination. Yes, this really happened. God certainly fought this battle for His people.

Let God fight your battles!

Three Little Words

Jesus was sound asleep. He had worked very hard that day, and now He was so tired He let His disciples row the boat while He took a much-needed nap.

Suddenly, a violent storm arose and threatened to sink the boat, which was quickly filling with water. The disciples tried to bail out the water. All seasoned fishermen, they worked hard but to no avail. The boat was in danger of sinking at any moment.

A flash of lightening revealed the Savior sound asleep in the mighty storm. Screaming for help, the men woke Jesus from His nap. As He looked around at the terror on their faces, and then up at the storm, He simply stood up and spoke three little words: "Peace, be still" (Mark 4:39). The storm dropped into the sea, and the sea became calm. The storm was over.

I am a witness to the fact that God has the capacity to still the storm from within each of us. Each personal storm is different. Sometimes the storm becomes a terrifying battle. Some inner storms are much milder. Yet, we all have a God who can and will give us the peace we long for if we only ask. Remember, He says, "Whatsoever ye shall ask in prayer, believing, ye shall receive" (Matt. 21:22).

Whatever storm is brewing in your heart and mind just now, turn it over to the Prince of peace. He may surprise you with these three little words: peace be still.

This story is just another reminder to let God fight your battles.

The Feet of Jesus

Weary after a day in the carpenter's shop, Jesus walked home. He had been standing on His feet all day long working for others. I can imagine Him singing as He worked, because He was full of courage and love.

As a young man in Joseph's carpenter shop, He made things out of wood, probably tables, chairs, window frames, cradles, doors—anything the people needed. His own family lived in a poor house in a little town called Nazareth.

Although He was Mary's son, He was also the Son of God. However, His divinity did not keep Him from the life and toil of a Jewish lifestyle. So He was weary at the end of the day, except of course on Sabbaths when He rested from His work.

When He was about 30 years of age, He traveled to the river Jordan to be baptized by John the Baptist. After His baptism, He went into the wilderness and lived there for forty days without food. At the end of this fast, He was tempted by the devil, but he passed each temptation (Matt. 4:1-11). After this experience, He started His ministry. As the Messiah, the Savior of the world, He spent the next three and a half years walking to various town and villages with His twelve disciples and teaching the people about the kingdom of God. Also, He healed people of their diseases, released them from demons, and restored sight and speech to those who could not see, hear, or speak.

As the Messiah, He was on His feet all day. His was a very busy life, sometimes crushed by the crowds of people wanting to be healed. There were others just wanting to get a glimpse of Him. And, oh yes, His enemies continually challenged Him. Yet, tired and weary from His work, He often climbed a hill just to be alone with His Father in heaven and pray for strength. His feet must have been very tired. Remember, He wore sandals, not comfortable walking shoes.

What wonderful times it must have been to visit Mary and Martha. They, along with their brother, Lazarus, opened their home and hearts to Jesus and His disciples from time to time.

How pleased Jesus was when Mary of Bethany chose to sit at the feet of Jesus. He said to her sister, "Mary hath chosen that good part" (Luke 10:42).

On another occasion, Mary kissed and anointed Jesus' feet at a banquet at Simon's home shortly before Jesus' death. The disciples were angered that so much money had been spent on the expensive ointment that soothed His feet, but He indicated, "She hath done what she could: she is come aforehand to anoint my body to the burying" (Mark 14:8). This was the only time when our Savior's feet were especially treasured.

Soon after that beautiful event, we find Jesus kneeling at the disciples' feet during the Last Supper in the upper room. Any of the disciples could have washed His feet, but instead, Jesus knelt down before each man and washed their feet. What humility—what humbleness. The beautiful chapter of John 13 describes the experience of Jesus washing their feet.

The next scene in Jesus' life was a trial before the Jewish leaders—a trial with trumped up charges that resulted in a sentence of death on the cross. As I read about the cruel way Jesus was condemned to die, my heart hurts for my Savior. He suffered beyond human measures, but He stayed on that cross, enduring incredible pain for you and for me (Luke 23).

But that was on Friday. The rest of the story is incredible glory. On Sunday He was resurrected from the dead. The good news is that death itself was not strong enough to keep our Savior in the grave. He is risen!

Just before He ascended back to heaven, His feet were the last part of His body to touch the earth. As He ascended, the disciples looked up in amazement, watching Him rise.

Someday soon He is returning again. Yes, scars will always be on Jesus' feet and in His hands, but those scars will be the most beautiful scars we will ever see.

The Bible tells us how to use our feet for Jesus. Romans 10:15 exclaims, "How beautiful are the feet of them that preach the gospel of peace."

Just imagine that our feet also have value for our Savior. Indeed, go, tell others about the Messiah, our Savior, our Lord, our King; yes, our very best Friend, Jesus Christ, is the promised Messiah.

The Hands of Jesus

Forming Adam from the earth must have been a great joy for Jesus. Dust and mud clung to His pure hands as He shaped Adam's body. Alongside the joy must have been the sorrow of the possibility of evil entering this perfect world He had just created. Jesus' hands were always blessing, always giving, always loving.

Yes, Adam was perfect; so was his wife, Eve. Yet, they gave into temptation, and evil began in the Garden of Eden, which changed everything (Gen. 3). Later in the history of the earth, God gave His people the Ten Commandments to guide people in life's choices.

These commandments were written in stone by the finger of the Lord in the presence of Moses. This event took place in the wilderness when the Lord was delivering His people from slavery in Egypt. These laws were to be a guideline for true living (Exod. 20:3-17).

Unfortunately, God's people chose to go their own way, ignoring the will of God and worshipping idols, gods of their own design. They had turned their backs on God for years. The entire Old Testament tells of the struggles the Israelites had simply because they did not obey the law of God.

The New Testament tells about Jesus' life and ministry. With His hands He blessed five loaves and two fishes. As He broke and blessed the bread and fishes, they multiplied right before the eyes of the people. His disciples distributed this bread and fish to 5,000 hungry men, plus woman and children.

We find Jesus putting His hands on the heads of the children, blessing them and loving them. His touch was important to the children and appreciated by the mothers (Matt. 19:13-15).

Jesus also healed with His hands. He touched the people, spoke to them, and they were healed. He often lifted up His hands to heaven when praying and when blessing people.

In my estimation the most awesome healings Jesus performed were with lepers. He always touched them. They were the "untouchables" in Israel. They were contagious. They were ostracized. Yet, these were the very ones He touched with His healing hands.

Jesus' touch was cleansing to the lepers (Matt. 8:3). His touch was healing to Peter's mother-in-law (Matt. 8:15). He gave sight to the blind as he touched their eyes (Matt. 9:29, 30). His was a reassuring, healing touch (Matt. 17:7; 20:34).

Near the end of Jesus' life on earth, Jesus washed the disciples' feet by hand. He touched and cleaned their dirty, dusty feet. He even washed the feet of Judas who was to betray Him into the hands of His enemies just hours later (John 13:4-10).

In the Garden of Gethsemane, Jesus restored the ear of Malchus, the high priest's servant. Peter had struck at Malchus with his sword and actually cut off his right ear. With a touch of the Master's hand, the ear was healed (Luke 22:50, 51).

After a phony trial, Jesus' hands were nailed cruelly to a wooden cross. He hung by His hands for six agonizing hours. He stayed on that cross for me and you.

After His resurrection Jesus appeared at dinner with His disciples. They couldn't figure out where He had gone. He was no longer in the grave, but no one knew where He was. Then, on Sunday night, He came to eat with them (Luke 24:36-40).

He showed His hands to them. They were astonished. They saw the scars, and they believed Jesus to be who He said He was—the Savior, the Son of God, the Messiah. They believed because they saw His hands.

The last time the disciples saw Jesus, He raised His hands and blessed them (Luke 24:50). Then He rose up and ascended into heaven to prepare a home for you and me. His hands are still active.

The Mouth of Jesus

"Let there be light." With these words, Jesus spoke this earth into being. For five days He spoke light, air, plants, grass and trees, sun, moon, and stars, and fish and birds into existence. Then on the sixth day He created animals and Adam and Eve. Once His work was over, He rested and called the seventh day the Sabbath, or the day of rest (Gen. 1 and 2).

After Creation, when the earth was perfect and totally beautiful, Jesus came down to earth from His heavenly home to walk and talk with Adam and Eve. What a special way to end the day, talking with God.

Unfortunately, when they ate the forbidden fruit and disobeyed God's command, they were forced to leave the Garden of Eden. After leaving the garden, Adam and Eve were blessed with the birth of Cain and Abel. But Cain had an evil heart. And the Lord warned Cain, "Sin lieth at the door" of your heart (Gen. 4:7). But he chose to not listen to God, and Cain killed Abel. Then God blessed Adam and Eve with another child—Seth was born to be the forerunner to the Messiah.

Many years later Enoch, a man who listened to God's voice, was taken to heaven and translated because of his close connection with the Lord. He did not spurn God's voice as so many in his generation were doing (Gen. 5:24).

Finally, evil became so bad that God decided to destroy the earth and all the sinners along with their sins. He looked for a person He could trust. And Noah was the man. The Lord told Noah how to build an ark, including all the dimensions. The Lord could talk to Noah because He listened (Gen. 6:8, 9).

Many years later, God talked to Moses in a burning bush. He told Moses to go down to Egypt and deliver His people from the slavery of the Pharaoh (Exod. 3:2-5). In fact, the Lord spoke to Moses all through that journey in the wilderness.

Moses was given the Ten Commandments. He was also given a set of instructions for building the tabernacle, a place of worship for the Israelites for their forty-year journey.

The Lord had personal conversations with patriarchs like Abraham, prophets like Daniel, kings like David, and numerous other people all recorded in the Old Testament.

King David had much to say about the mouth of God—the words of God and the speech of God. "Thy word have I hid in mine heart" (Ps. 119:11).

Reaching into the New Testament, we first find Jesus speaking at the age of 12 in the temple with the leaders of the chosen people of God. He questioned the religious doctors, and His answers astounded the men (Luke 2:46, 47).

His incredible obedience to His earthly parents is surprising, as He had just learned who He was—the Son of God, the Savior, the Messiah, the Lamb of God (Luke 2:49-52). The next eighteen years of His life, he spent working as a carpenter and learning the Scriptures.

However, shortly after John the Baptist baptized Jesus, He chose twelve men to be His disciples, and He began His life work. One of His best-known sermons is the Sermon on the Mount, or the Beatitudes. These blessings teach us the best way to live (Matt. 5:3-12).

With His mouth, Jesus spent three and a half years preaching, teaching, and healing. He spoke. He used His mouth without fear of the consequences of His words. He spoke truth to those who would listen. The leaders of Israel did all they could to trick and trap Him, but again and again Jesus' speech was opposite from what the religious leaders expected, and they finally succeeded in silencing Him by death on the cross.

Jesus spoke seven last words while hanging on the cross. Crying out with a loud voice, He said, "My God, my God, why hast thou forsaken me?" (Matt. 27:46).

Jesus also made the following statements while on the cross right before He died:

"Father, forgive them; for they know not what they do" (Luke 23:34).

To the thief on the other cross, He said, "Verily I say unto thee, Today shalt thou be with me in Paradise" (Luke 23:43).

"Father, into thy hands I commend my spirit" (Luke 23:46).

Turning toward Mary, His mother, He said, "Woman, behold thy son!" To John, He commissioned, "Behold thy mother!" (John 19:26, 27).

"It is finished" (John 19:30).

After His death and resurrection, He told His disciples, and all who believe in Him, to go and tell others about Him (Matt. 28:19, 20).

The Eyes of Jesus

Jesus wept. As Jesus looked over the city of Jerusalem, His eyes filled with tears. At a time when He might have been extremely happy, He cried.

Why did Jesus cry? Was He afraid of His coming death? Absolutely not. Was He afraid of the leaders of the synagogue? No, of course not. He stood up to them again and again, speaking truth against their accusing lies. Was He afraid of failure? That could have happened, but it didn't. His complete trust in His Father took that fear from Him. So why did Jesus cry?

As He stood at the top of the hill looking down over the temple of Jerusalem, He saw His people, the very ones He was to die for that very week. He saw the temple filled with those who were chosen to be His own people. He looked beyond and saw down through the centuries to all His people. He looked at you and me through liquid eyes. He, the Savior of all, cried for all those who would reject His free gift.

Jesus wept over Jerusalem. Luke 19:28-44 documents the story of Jesus riding into Jerusalem on a donkey. The people thought to proclaim Him king of the Jews, not realizing that He was already King of the universe.

Thy cried out, "Blessed be the King that cometh in the name of the Lord: peace in heaven, and glory in the highest" (Luke 19:38). Verse 41 then says, "And when he was come near, he beheld the city, and wept over it."

He could see with His eyes the tragic reality of His chosen people choosing the wrong way, choosing to follow the devil's directions, choosing to turn their backs on Him in just a few days. This sorrow was not for Himself. It was for each of us. His tears, filling His eyes and overflowing down His holy cheeks, were not in vain if we simply choose Jesus as our Savior, our King. And we delight to have Him as our very best Friend.

This was not the only time sadness was in Jesus' voice. Matthew 23:37 describes His sadness at the deplorable depth His chosen people sank to. "O Jerusalem, Jerusalem, thou that killest the prophets, and stonest them which are sent unto thee, how often would I have gathered thy children together, even as a hen gathereth her chickens under her wings, and ye would not!" These thoughts had to hurt Him deeply.

Jesus again cried when His close friend Lazarus died. Martha and her sister, Mary, had just told Jesus of their brother's death, and He groaned and was troubled (John 11:33). Then "Jesus wept" (verse 35).

When I was a child, and we had to repeat a memory verse from the Bible, we all raised our hands and offered to say the shortest verse in the Bible; John 11:35 was the prize text. However, in our childishness, we little realized the importance attached to this text. Our Savior really truly cried; He felt sadness as we do.

This time Jesus' tears were not for Jerusalem. His tears were shed at the tomb of Lazarus. He felt the pain of the sisters. Our Savior hasn't changed. He still feels the pain and tears of each of us.

As He prayed at the tomb, He talked to His Father, saying, "And I knew that thou hearest me always: but because of the people which stand by I said it, that they may believe that thou hast sent me" (verse 42).

The eyes of Jesus are the same eyes that 2 Chronicles 16:9 describes. "The eyes of the Lord run to and fro throughout the whole earth." He sees us as He goes about His heavenly work. He is watching over all of us. He wants the very best for each of us. Just believe.

This next verse may be a comfort and blessing to some and terrifying for others: "The eyes of the Lord are in every place, beholding the evil and the good" (Prov. 15:3).

Jeremiah, a great Old Testament prophet, declares the following in his book: "For I will set mine eyes upon them for good" (Jer. 24:6). What a wonderful promise for each of us.

Jesus' eyes, God's eyes, the eyes of the Lord are a blessing.

The Heart of Jesus

The mystery of the virgin birth is beyond human understanding. Jesus was conceived in Mary by the Holy Spirit for a very special purpose. He had a mission on earth to save the world.

The fulfillment of the plan of salvation began to take shape in Mary's womb, developing over a period of nine months as any other normal baby. His first heartbeat was discernable in approximately twenty-one days. His human heart was completely formed in eight weeks.

He was truly a special Baby. However, He grew within the womb as all babies grow. He was a perfect Child, and Scripture tells us that He grew "in wisdom and stature, and in favour with God and man" (Luke 2:52).

His heart turned toward His people once He was a grown man. He loved them so much that He gave His thoughts, His time, His complete concentration, and finally His heart to all people on the cross. He died, not from exhaustion, but from a broken heart.

As our hearts turn toward family, friends, or other people we hold dear, let us remember that Jesus has a heart of love for us. Have you ever heard the children's song "Jesus Loves Me"? "Jesus loves me this I know. For the Bible tells me so.... Yes, Jesus loves me. Yes, Jesus loves me. Yes, Jesus loves me. The Bible tells me so."

Jesus gave His heart for you. Why not give Him the only true gift there is—your heart.

The Christ of the Cross

I wrote the following in an effort to connect my thoughts on the important concept of Christ's love for us and His death.

Home is where your *heart* is.
From the heart comes *love*.
The ultimate love came from the *cross*.

113

The cross is where Christ paid the penalty for our *sin*.
Sin is separation from *God*.
God is our *Creator*.
Indeed, people are created in the very *image* of God.

Some people say, "God can't be *proved*."
Perhaps that's true. But God can be *experienced*.
Experience with God comes from *need*.
When we need God enough, *trust* begins
"In God we trust" is on every penny in our country.
Why is it so difficult for some people to find that trust?

Looking at the cross of Jesus, there is *forgiveness*.
Looking at the cross of Jesus, we find *ultimate love*.
Looking at the cross of Jesus, there is *eternal life*.

There's power in the *blood*.
Blood is hard to talk about, but it's *saving blood*.
What are we *saved* for?
Eternal life of pure *joy* and *delight*.
Every *need* and *want* will be met.
Look to the cross, *accept* your Savior, *live* forever.
God bless you now and always

Sad Beginning—Happy Ending

Two tearful men were walking out of Jerusalem toward a town called Emmaus. As they cried, walked, and tried to talk, a stranger caught up with them. As the three men continued their journey, the third man, the stranger, asked the other two why they were so sad and perplexed.

It was a Sunday night; Jesus had just been crucified that weekend on Friday. They had hoped He was the deliverer the Jews had been expecting. Then on Friday their hopes were dashed on the cross.

Yet, as they shared their thoughts with the stranger, they explained their perplexity about what they had just heard. Jesus had died on Friday; yet there was a buzz in Jerusalem that He had risen on Sunday morning. Perplexed and painfully sad, they were curious as to why this stranger hadn't heard the tragic news. They had been trying to sort out the details and rumors when the stranger had joined their conversation.

It is not recorded what the stranger quoted, but we do have hints. Starting with Moses, He quoted Old Testament scriptures about Himself. One prophet after another prophesied about the Messiah.

Nearing Emmaus, the sun was setting, so they invited the stranger to spend the night with them. He agreed. They ate supper together. As He was about to bless the bread, His hands revealed fresh scars where nails had pierced His flesh only three days before. They finally recognized their Lord. Yes, the stranger was Jesus Christ who had been crucified on Friday, had rested on Sabbath, and had risen from the dead on Sunday.

As Jesus left the scene, they exclaimed, "Did not our heart burn within us ... while he opened to us the scriptures?" (Luke 24:32). Indeed, to be with Jesus, even now in the twenty-first century, more than two thousand years later, our hearts still "burn within" as we contemplate the gift of eternal life Jesus gave us on the cross.

Christ is the center of all times, all events, and every deep thought we can have. Jesus Christ fulfilled the Old Testament prophecies about His birth, life, death, and resurrection. You may be interested in some of these very texts.

Christ—The Fulfillment of Prophecy

- Genesis 3:15
- Psalms 22, 34, 41, 78, 118
- Isaiah 7, 40, 42, 53, 61
- Micah 5
- Zechariah 9, 11, 12, 13
- Malachi 3
- Matthew 1:22; 2:15, 23; 4:14; 8:17; 13:35; 21:4; 26:56; 27:35
- Mark 14:27; 15:34
- Luke 21:22; 24:44
- John 12:38; 15:25; 17:12; 19:24
- Acts 3:18; 13:29

Jesus' Predictions About His Timing

- Mark 1:15—"The time is fulfilled, and the kingdom of God is at hand."

Jesus' Predictions About His Sufferings

- Mark 8:31; Luke 9:22—Jesus predicted that He would suffer, be rejected, be killed, and rise again after three days.

Jesus' Predictions About His Death

- John 7:33—"Yet a little while am I with you, and then I go unto him that sent me."
- John 13:33—"Whither I go, ye cannot come."
- John 14:28—"I go away ,and come again unto you."
- John 16:5—"None of you asketh me, Whither goest thou?"

Jesus' Predictions About His Resurrection

- Matthew 16:21—"Raised again the third day."
- Matthew 26:32—"After I am risen again, I will go before you into Galilee."
- John 2:19—"Destroy this temple, and in three days I will raise it up."
- Jesus' Predictions About His Words
- Luke 21:33—"My words shall not pass away."

To Die For

"You simply must have some pie. It's to *die* for," gushed my friend. And, indeed it was luscious. Licking my lips, my mind started whirling.

I had an eating plan that did not include *pie*. So, I asked myself silently, "Why pie?" Salad, soup, and lots of greens—persistence and patience eating those kinds of things just don't have the same enticement.

Each of the Ten Commandments of the Lord has a benefit passed down from the throne of grace if only we would obey as God wants us to.

So how does pie fit into God's laws in my life? Ah, yes, the sixth commandment says, "Thou shalt not kill" (Exod. 20:13). Some translations say, "Thou shall not murder." How do I figure that "pie to die for" comes under this category? Is anything on earth really worth dying for, especially a piece of pie? If only my size was normal and I had not eaten so many to-die-for pies before, perhaps this piece would not have troubled me. But this piece did make me think. Do I really love life as I say I do? Oh, yes, I do.

To die for—this expression actually began in heaven before the world was created when Jesus agreed to lay down His life if humanity failed the test and disobeyed the Father's commands to not eat from the tree of knowledge of good and evil.

God wanted His created beings to have the freedom of worshiping Him, or not. It was a huge risk, but a plan was in place should they choose the wrong path.

Of course, we find in Genesis 3 the story of Adam and Eve's wrong choice. The serpent, which was Satan, tempted Eve with "to-die-for fruit." The problem is that the fruit he offered really brought death—not immediately, but upon that first bite, sin entered the world and death was present.

Fortunately, God had a plan to save His fallen creatures in the form of His Son. Dying on a wretched cross took the guilt of our sin. What a God! What a Savior! We don't have to die because we have a Savior who offered His body to die for you and me.

The Alabaster Box

The aroma of a highly fragrant ointment quickly filled the banquet hall as Mary broke the alabaster box of spikenard. This powerful perfume represented about a year's wages. The Savior was being especially honored by Mary, a former prostitute, before His death. Jesus had rebuked the demons that plagued her seven times. Gratitude flowed from every cell in her body. Jesus had also forgiven her when the Pharisees caught her in the very act of breaking the seventh commandment.

Her Savior had asked, "Where are those thine accusers? hath no man condemned thee?" Looking around she replied, "No man, Lord." His loving assurance, "Neither do I condemn thee: go, and sin no more" (John 8:10, 11) must have been the most beautiful words one could ever hear. Since the men were ready to stone her for her sin, Jesus' words at that time changed her life.

This same Mary returned to her brother Lazarus' home and lived a quiet life with him and their sister, Martha. This same Mary sat at the feet of Jesus, listening to His voice as He detailed His approaching death (Luke 10:39). And after He died, she was first at the tomb (John 20:1) and first to talk to Jesus after His resurrection (John 20:11-18). Her spiritual life had been healed, and her gratitude was enormous.

Lazarus and Martha played a major part in Simon's banquet. Jesus had just raised Lazarus from the dead, so he was seated beside Jesus as an honored guest. Martha served the meal. I suspect Mary was not invited, because she quietly gained entrance into the banquet room and quickly sat at Jesus' feet once more. This time, she was not there to listen to Him, but to honor Him.

Pouring the perfumed ointment over Jesus' head, she then sat on the floor and let her tears wash His feet. She then anointed His feet with the ointment and wiped them with her hair. She planned to be quiet about this act, but the perfume filled the room.

Instead of enjoying the aroma, two men had their noses pushed out of joint.

Simon, the host, privately thought that if Jesus knew what kind of sinner Mary was He wouldn't even let her touch Him. Previously, Jesus had healed Simon from leprosy. Simon's gesture of gratitude led him to honor Jesus with this banquet. However, Simon's gratitude fell short of the deep thankfulness of Mary's; his heart was filled with sharp criticism of Jesus and Mary.

Judas, on the other hand, was quite outspoken. He blurted out that this money should have been given to the poor. He called Mary's act "a waste."

I can just see Mary cringe on the floor, perhaps just like she had done when accused of adultery. And, as the other disciples picked up Judas' put-down, Jesus said, "Leave her alone … she has done a beautiful thing to me" (Mark 14:6, NIV).

Jesus, picking up the attitude in the room, stated that this would be a memorial for all who hear the gospel. Reading Simon's mind, Jesus told another story. Asking who had more gratitude, a large debtor or a small debtor?

Simon saw through his selfish attitude. However, greed darkened Judas' heart, and he went out and sold His Savior for just thirty pieces of silver—a paltry sum compared to the perfume. Possibly he wanted things to hurry up, making Jesus King over Israel, making him the logical treasurer in Jesus' kingdom. Not knowing how far off he was, ultimately, this selfish act led to his suicide later that very week. Simon, on the other hand, became a firm believer in and a true disciple of his Savior.

This wonderful story demonstrates that greed, selfishness, an accusing attitude, jealousy, and pride push God away. But a tender, loving, caring, and thankful heart allows God to do His work from the inside, ultimately leading to eternal life.

To read the complete story of Mary's unselfish gift to her Master, turn to one of the following passages: Matthew 26:6-13; Mark 14:3-11; Luke 7:36-50; or John 12:1-11.

Cock-A-Doodle-Doo

The rooster crowed for the second time. Then Peter remembered Jesus' words: "Before the cock crow twice, thou shalt deny me thrice" (Mark 14:30).

To be spotted out in a noisy mob was too much for Peter. Watching his Friend Jesus, the Messiah, in trial overcame Peter, and as two maidens and a servant of the high priest pointed him out as "one of them," he lost it. "I know not the man," he said (Matt. 26:74).

Just then, the rooster crowed. Peter's mind snapped to the present, and he realized that the Savior had warned him just hours before that he would deny Him.

He must have frozen for a moment as he realized what he had done. Then he did the right thing. He fixed his eyes on Jesus Christ. As he did, Jesus turned his direction and looked straight at Peter. Their eyes locked. I cannot imagine the horror he must have felt as Jesus looked at him.

But true to form, there was no condemnation in Jesus' eyes. Right there in the middle of this false trial that Jesus was enduring, the look in Jesus' eyes broke Peter's arrogance, and he left the trial hall in bitter tears.

The look. What must it have been? Check out Ellen White's description in *The Desire of Ages*: "The Saviour turned ... and looked full upon His poor disciple. At the same time Peter's eyes were drawn to his Master. In that gentle countenance he read deep pity and sorrow, but there was no anger there" (p. 713).

John 3:17 tells us that "God sent not his Son into the world to condemn the world; but that the world through him might be saved." Peter was converted, changed, that instant.

There comes a moment when each of us must look to Christ, realizing that by the way we have lived, each one of us has denied our Lord. He is the same loving, forgiving Savior today as He was while walking the earth.

Daddy, Why Did You Leave Me?

In extreme pain, emotional as well as physical, Jesus deeply felt the absence of the Father. It broke His heart. However, the Father had to turn away and let Jesus bear our sins on the cross alone. The sin was so great that the Father could not be in its presence.

Jesus cried with a loud voice, "My God, my God, why hast thou forsaken me?" (Mark 15:34). Just hours before, Jesus had prayed in the Garden of Gethsemane, "Abba, Father, all things are possible unto thee; take away this cup from me: nevertheless not what I will, but what thou wilt" (Mark 14:36).

Imagine the six lonely hours He hung on the cross. The only person to even acknowledge that He was the Son of God was a thief on the cross next to Him. His own followers and His own mother were crying as they helplessly watched from a distance. All the other people shouted and ridiculed Him, taunting Him with scathing language for hours.

Then, looking up, He inquired of His Father, His God, His Daddy, the only One who could help Him: "Daddy, why did You leave Me?"

Twice before during Jesus' earthly ministry God had declared: "This is My beloved Son." But now, there was silence from God, His Father, His Daddy.

We all have probably experienced silence from our daddies, and possibly from God. However, God never leaves us; even when He is silent, He is always there.

But for the Savior, at the most difficult time of His life, silence loomed. "Daddy, why did You leave Me?" What great agony He felt as He hung there for my stupid sins, for your sins, indeed for a whole world of sin. He stayed there even though He felt deserted. He endured the silence from His Daddy for you and me. What a Savior!

The Lord Is Alive!

When Jesus said, "It is finished" (John 19:30), a new beginning was set in motion. Just two days later, "He is risen!" rang through the air, and the followers of Jesus stopped shedding tears and started shouting, "He's alive. Jesus is alive!"

Buddha, Confucius, Mohammed, and many religious leaders are in the grave. But our Savior is alive! This sets Christianity apart from all other religions. Our Creator, Redeemer, and Savior lives—and that makes all the difference.

When He left earth to return to His Father's throne, He left us with the most encouraging words: "Lo, I am with you always" (Matt. 28:20). In every act, with every word, even a glance of the eye, the Lord notices. When once the heart is turned toward Him, all things are right, all things are changed from within. He truly is with you right now.

Is the Lord alive in your heart? If not, give it a thought just now. All things will be better. Although you may have a difficult time getting it right, He will be with you as you face the tough situations in your life. He will not leave you.

Jesus Is In Jail

I was talking to three female inmates a few months ago, and they all glowed with the presence of the Lord. Their faces actually shone. They all expressed that, "Jesus is in jail." We had a long talk about their future.

Each girl had a different story, of course. One was to get out of jail the following week. Being the teacher I am, I couldn't help asking what she was going to do once the last door clanged behind her, and she was outside. She laughed and said, "I have no plans."

We talked quite a while. I expressed that for her, Jesus was in jail, but did she expect to take Him with her in the outside world or leave Him behind? Grabbing her Bible, she said, "This I will take with me." She had learned to pray and had a strong conviction that God would lead, no matter her past, but she wasn't sure where she wanted to go. Finally, she said, "I do have an aunt in California who loves me and believes in me. She told me to come any time. I'll call her and go to her home."

The second girl was going to continue to be in jail for a bit longer, so she had more time to think about her future when she would get out. We also talked quite a bit. Her family didn't want her, but she had a degree and felt certain she could get a job.

The third girl was the one most aglow with the Lord's presence. She said, "I have my trial next week. They either will let me go free, or I will be sent to the penitentiary for twenty years."

I swallowed hard and asked, "Either way, do you plan to take Jesus with you?"

Her reply was encouraging to me. She said, "Either way, God will be my God no matter what. I have no fear."

Some of you who are reading this book will be out of jail or prison soon. I'll ask you, too: "Do you have a plan?"

If you have been reading *Peace in Prison*, I know you know about God's love for you. What are your plans with Jesus? Are you taking Him with you? Or will you leave Him behind? Have you accepted His free gift of salvation?

I wrote this book because I really care about you, but Jesus cares a whole lot more than I ever can. Jesus created you, redeemed your life on the cross, and is coming back very soon, sooner than we think. Now is the time to fall on your knees and say, "God, I need a Savior." Ask God for Jesus. It can't hurt, but it can heal. May God always bless you!

We invite you to view the complete
selection of titles we publish at:

www.TEACHServices.com

Scan with your mobile
device to go directly
to our website.

Please write or email us your praises, reactions,
or thoughts about this or any other book we publish at:

TEACH Services, Inc.
P U B L I S H I N G

www.TEACHServices.com

P.O. Box 954
Ringgold, GA 30736

info@TEACHServices.com

TEACH Services, Inc., titles may be purchased in bulk for
educational, business, fund-raising, or sales promotional use.
For information, please e-mail:

BulkSales@TEACHServices.com

Finally, if you are interested in seeing
your own book in print, please contact us at

publishing@TEACHServices.com

We would be happy to review your manuscript for free.

CPSIA information can be obtained at www.ICGtesting.com
Printed in the USA
LVOW112013230912

299896LV00001B/2/P

9 781572 588172